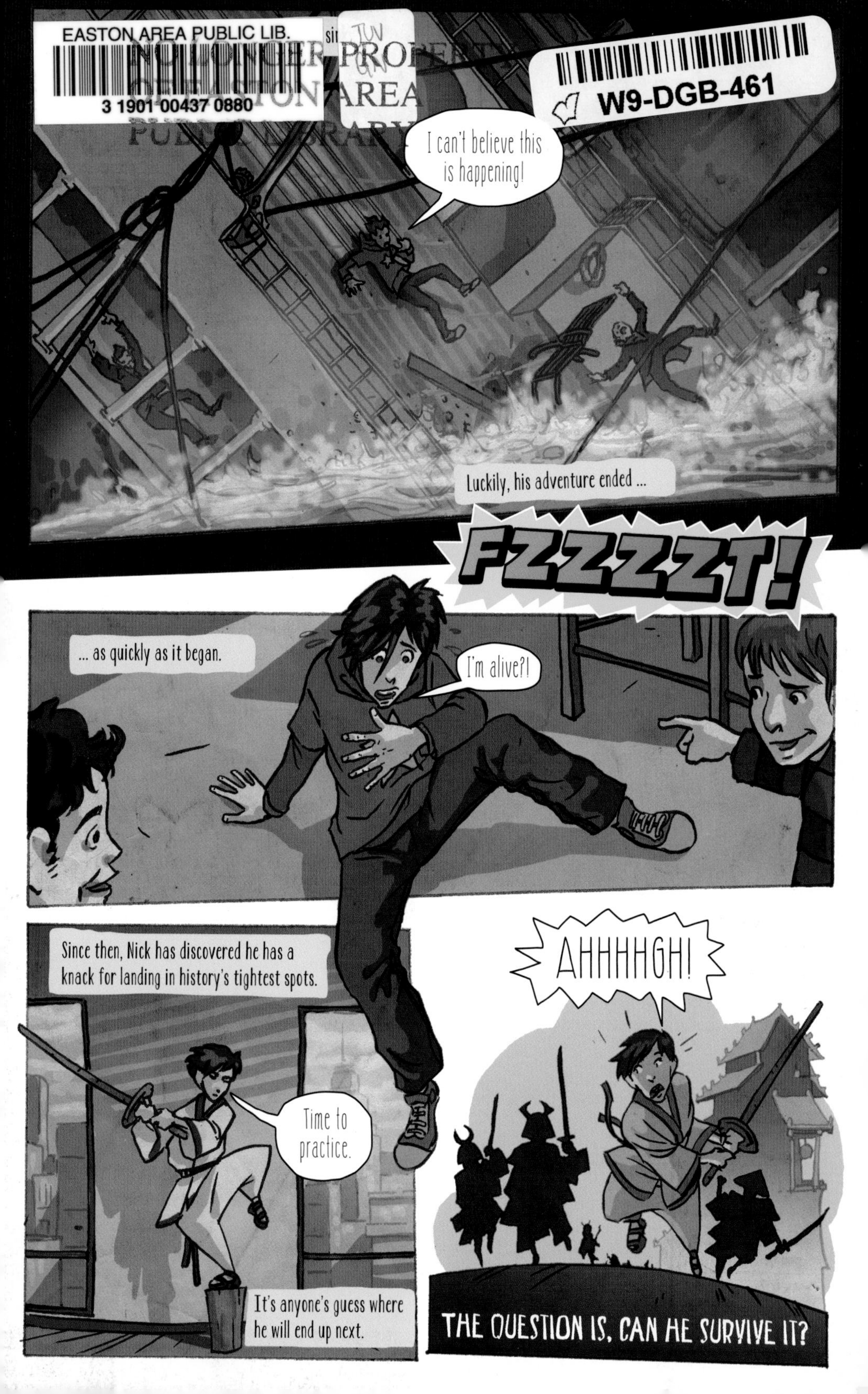
I can't believe this is happening!
Luckily, his adventure ended ...
FZZZZT!
... as quickly as it began.
I'm alive?!
Since then, Nick has discovered he has a knack for landing in history's tightest spots.
Time to practice.
It's anyone's guess where he will end up next.
AHHHHGH!
THE QUESTION IS, CAN HE SURVIVE IT?

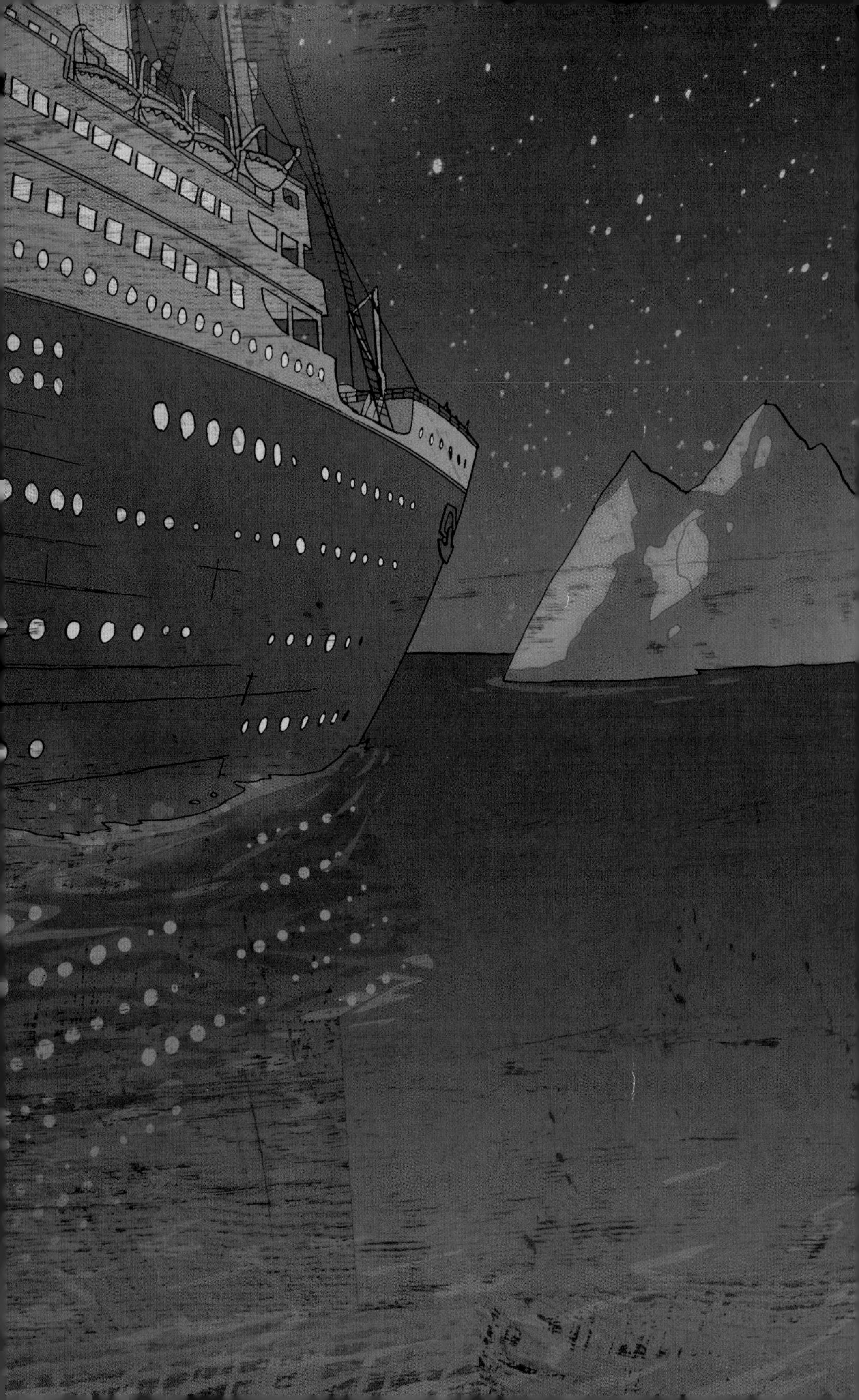

Nickolas Flux HISTORY CHRONICLES

TITANIC DISASTER!

NICKOLAS FLUX and the Sinking of the Great Ship

BY Nel Yomtov

ILLUSTRATED BY Mark Simmons

CONSULTANT: Richard Bell, PhD
Associate Professor of History
University of Maryland, College Park

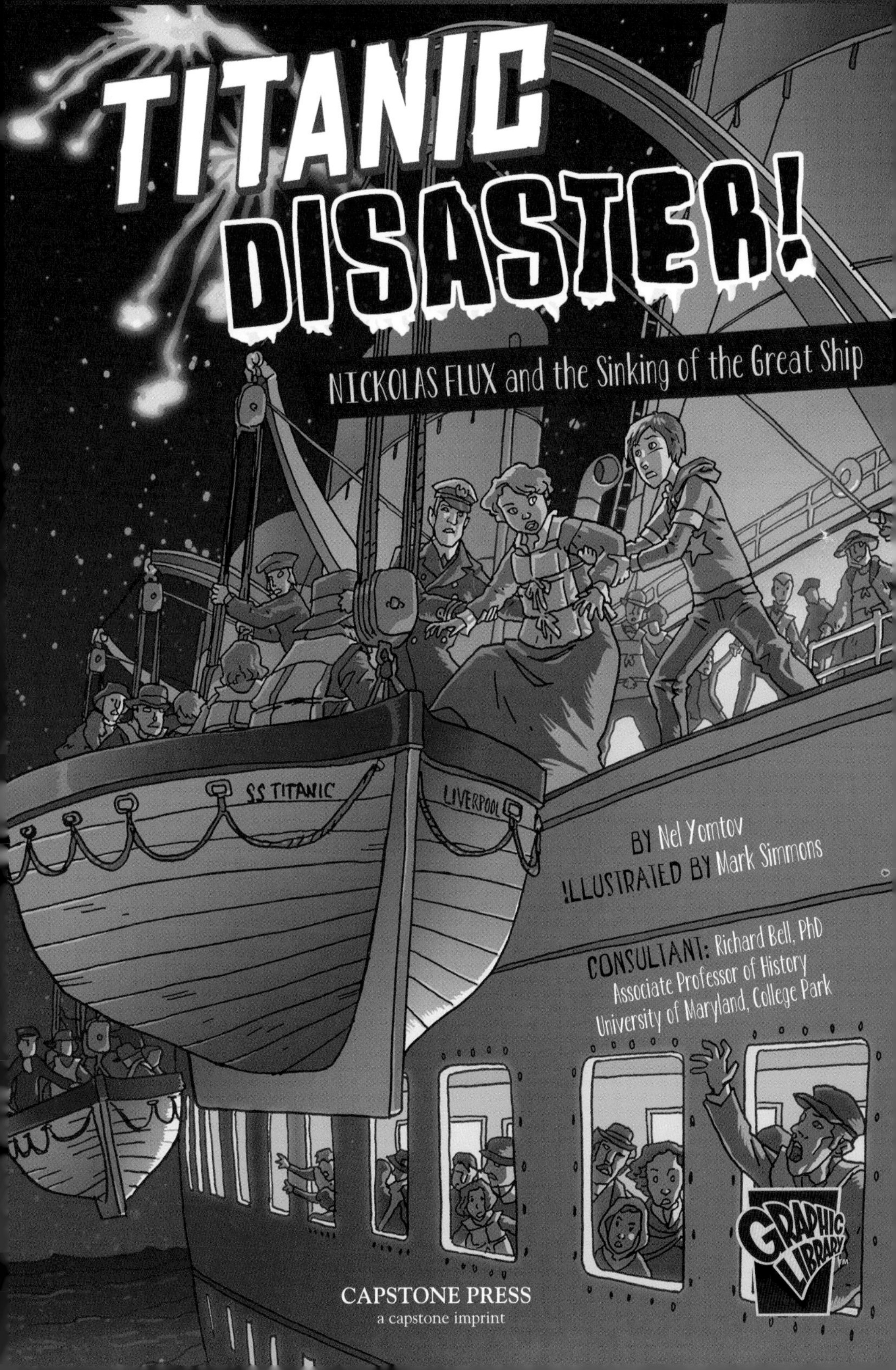

SS TITANIC
LIVERPOOL
GRAPHIC LIBRARY

CAPSTONE PRESS
a capstone imprint

Graphic Library is published by Capstone Press,
1710 Roe Crest Drive, North Mankato, Minnesota 56003
www.capstonepub.com

Library of Congress Cataloging-in-Publication Data
Yomtov, Nelson.
 Titanic disaster! : Nickolas Flux and the sinking of the great ship / by
Nel Yomtov.
    pages cm.—(Nickolas Flux history chronicles)
  Summary: "When a spontaneous time leap sends Nickolas Flux back
to the Titanic's maiden voyage, what's a teenage history buff to do? Try
to avoid going down with the ship, of course! From trying to help spot
icebergs to getting off the sinking ship safely, Nick must survive one of
the most disastrous events of the early 1900s"—Provided by publisher
 Includes bibliographical references.
  ISBN 978-1-4914-2070-6 (library binding)
  ISBN 978-1-4914-2286-1 (paperback)
  ISBN 978-1-4914-2288-5 (eBook PDF)
 1. Titanic (Steamship)—Juvenile fiction. [1. Titanic (Steamship)—
Fiction. 2. Ocean liners—Fiction. 3. Shipwrecks—Fiction. 4.
Time travel—Fiction.] I. Title.
 PZ7.7.Y66Ti 2015
 741.5'973—dc23   2014019588

Photo Credits:
Design Elements: Shutterstock (backgrounds)

Editor's note:
Direct quotations, noted in red type, appear on the following pages:
Pages 18, 26, and 31 from *Titanic: Voices from the Disaster* by Deborah
Hopkinson (New York: Scholastic, 2012).

EDITOR
Adrian Vigliano

ART DIRECTOR
Nathan Gassman

DESIGNER
Ashlee Suker

PRODUCTION SPECIALIST
Kathy McColley

Printed in the United States of America in Stevens Point, Wisconsin.
092014   008479WZS15

TABLE OF CONTENTS

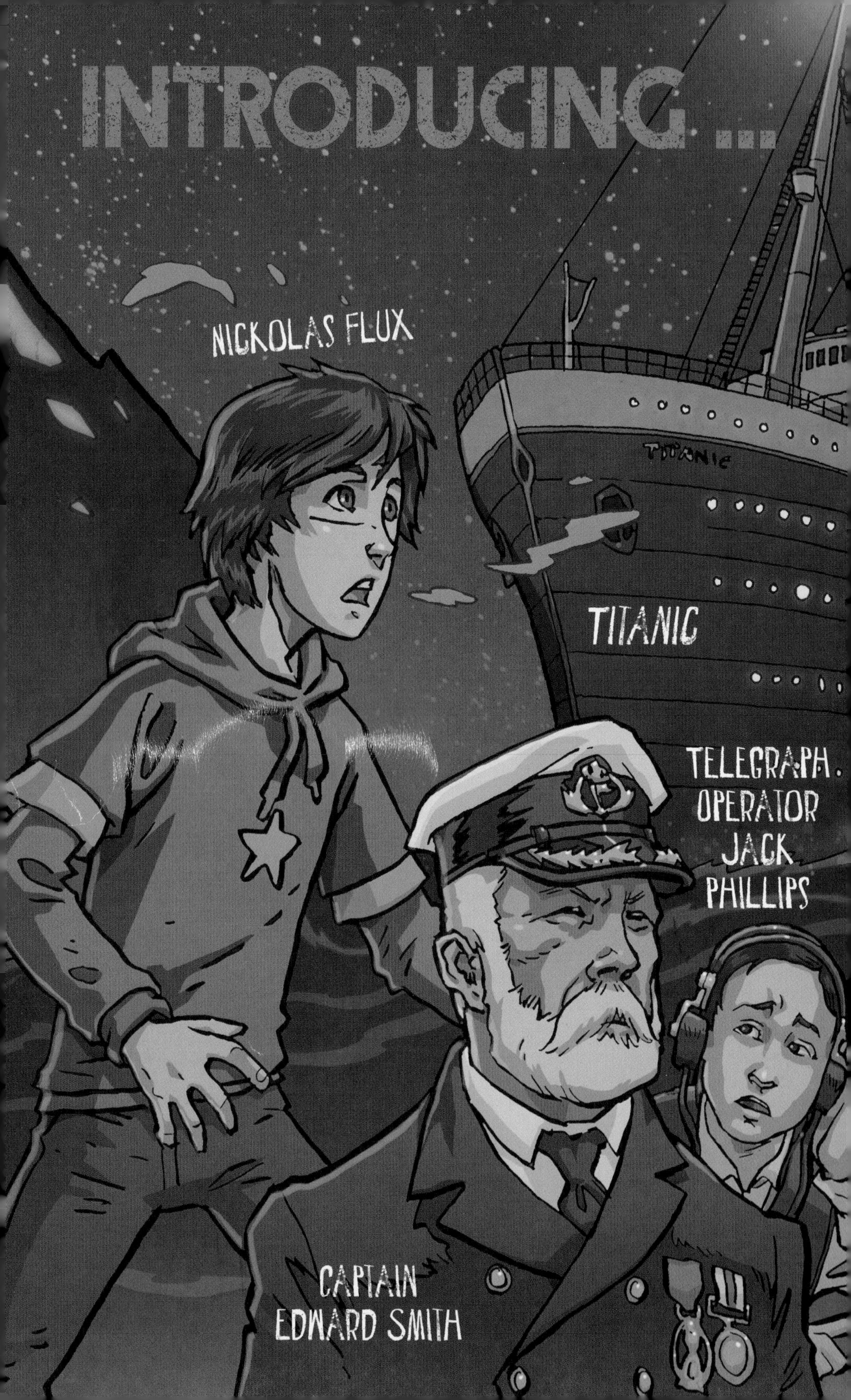
INTRODUCING ...
NICKOLAS FLUX
TITANIC
TITANIC
TELEGRAPH OPERATOR JACK PHILLIPS
CAPTAIN EDWARD SMITH

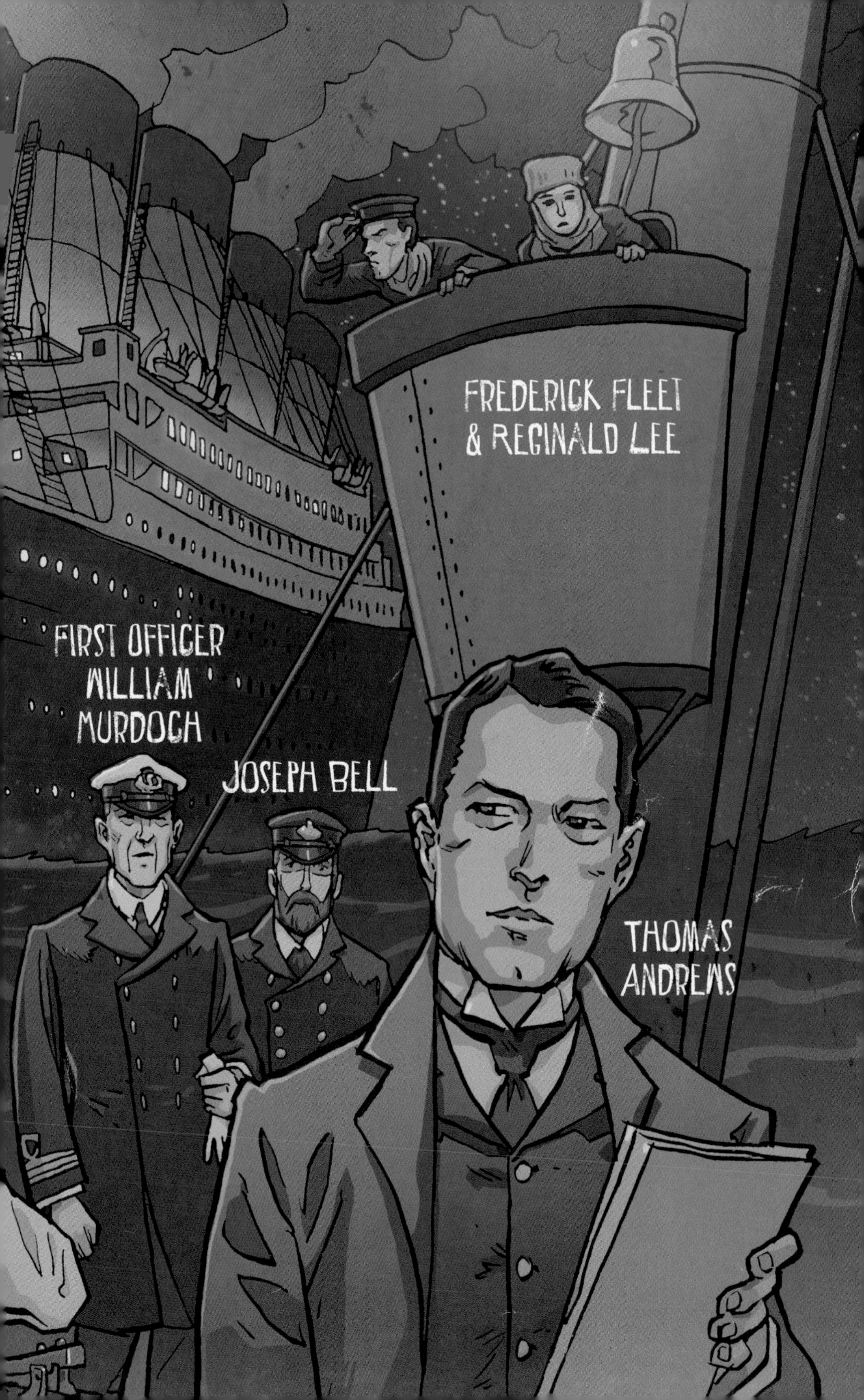
FREDERICK FLEET
& REGINALD LEE
FIRST OFFICER
WILLIAM
MURDOCH
JOSEPH BELL
THOMAS
ANDREWS

CHAPTER ONE
SCIENCE LAB

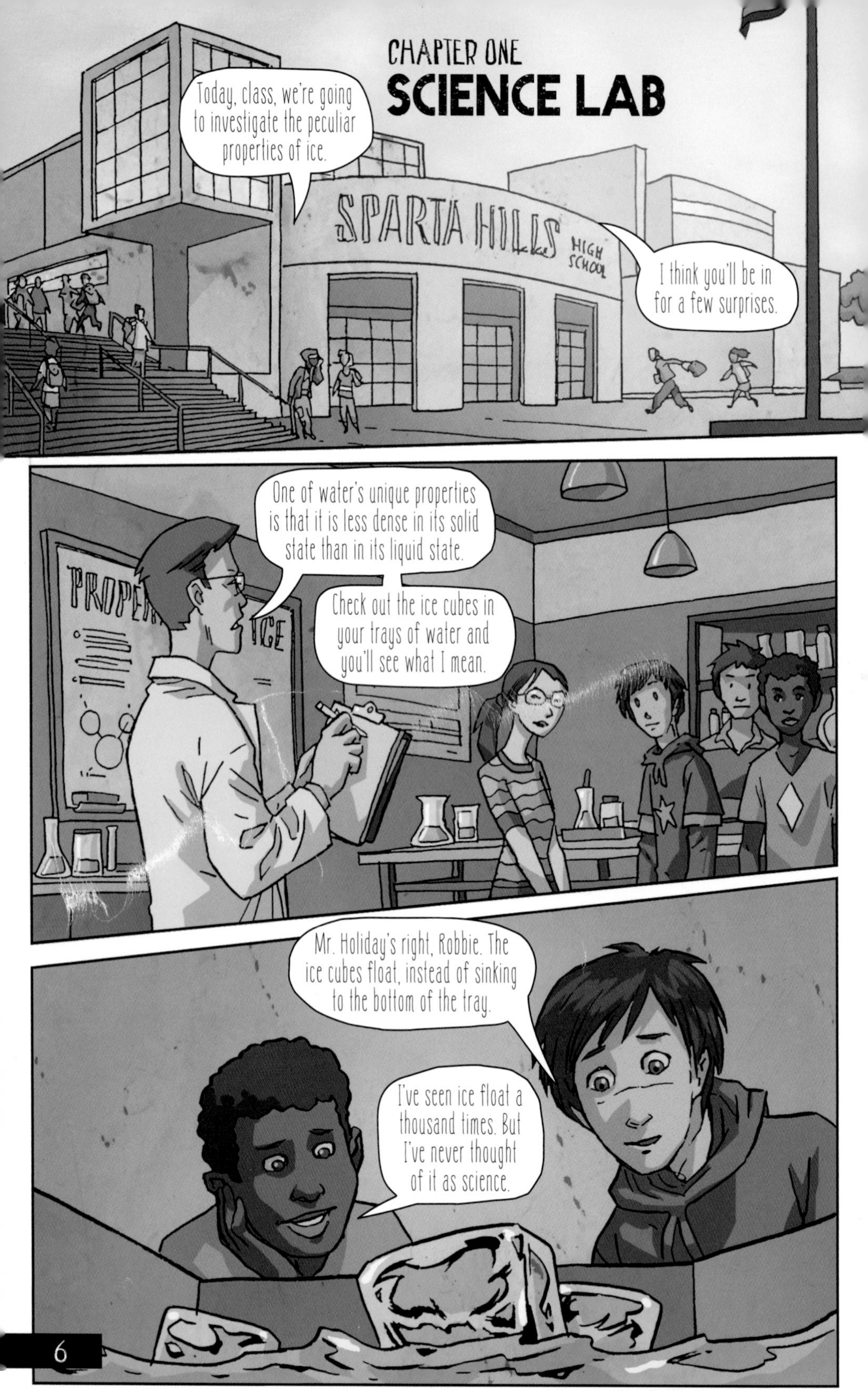
Today, class, we're going to investigate the peculiar properties of ice.
SPARTA HILLS HIGH SCHOOL
I think you'll be in for a few surprises.
One of water's unique properties is that it is less dense in its solid state than in its liquid state.
Check out the ice cubes in your trays of water and you'll see what I mean.
Mr. Holiday's right, Robbie. The ice cubes float, instead of sinking to the bottom of the tray.
I've seen ice float a thousand times. But I've never thought of it as science.

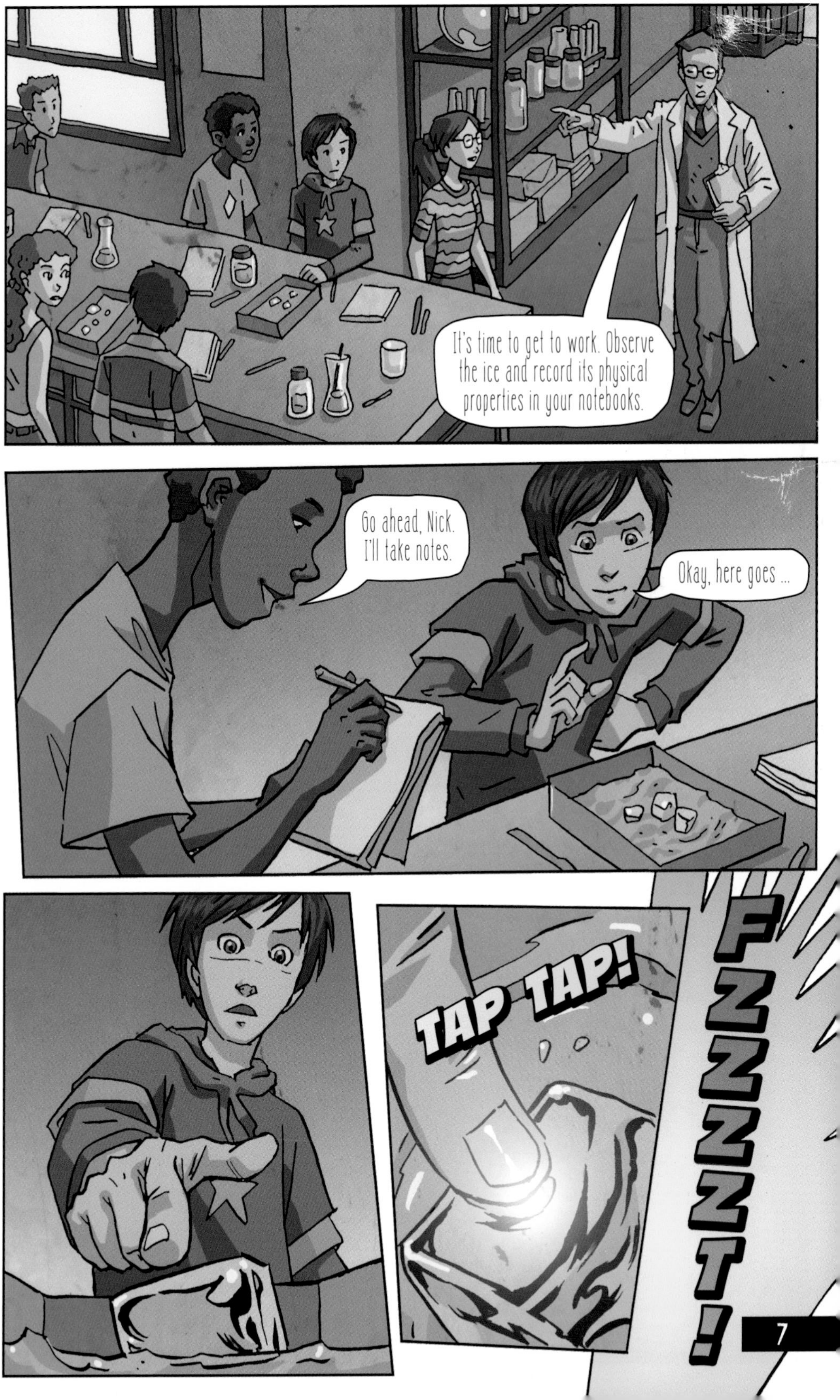

It's time to get to work. Observe the ice and record its physical properties in your notebooks.
Go ahead, Nick. I'll take notes.
Okay, here goes ...
TAP TAP!
FZZZZT!

CHAPTER TWO
SHIP OF DREAMS

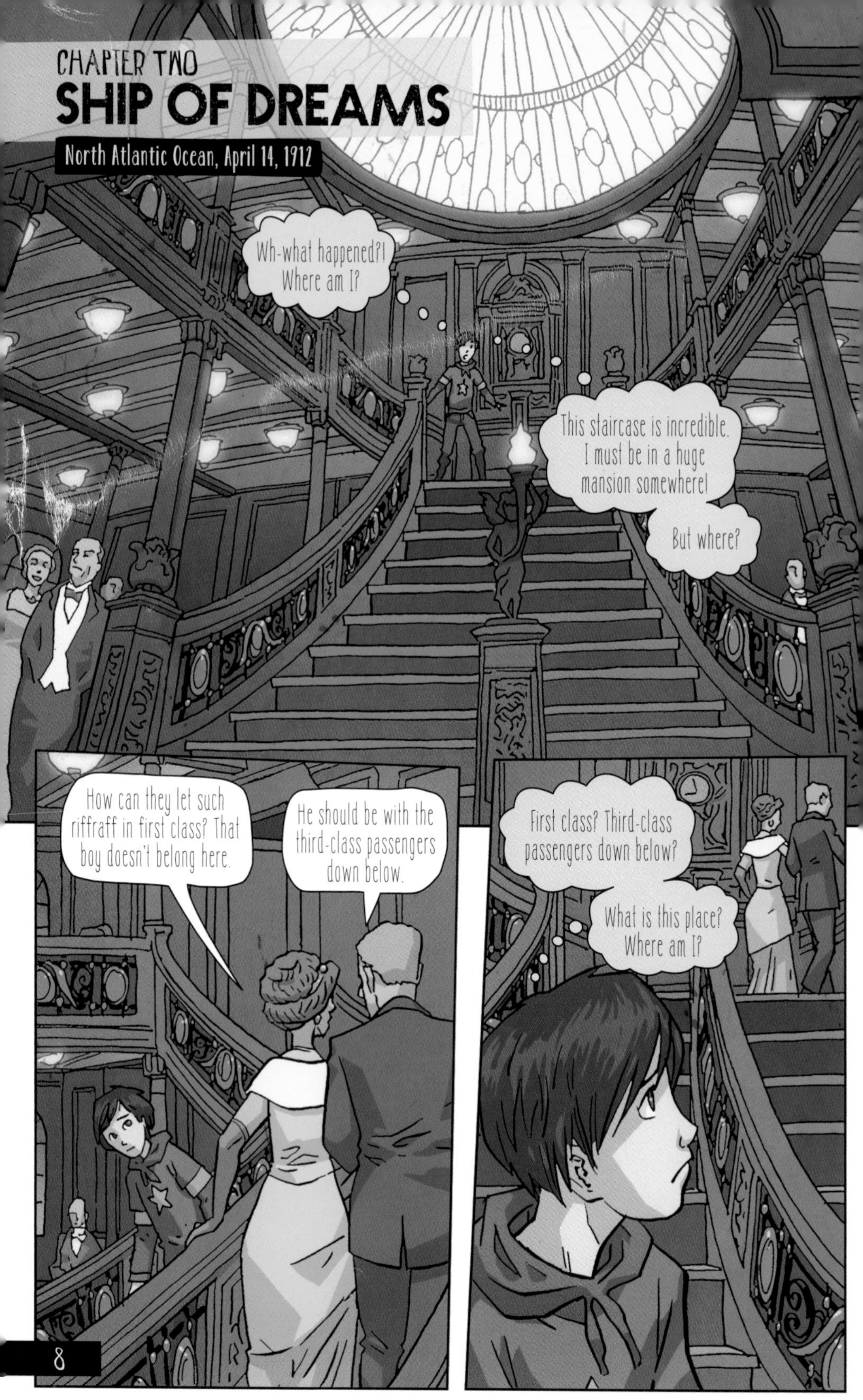
North Atlantic Ocean, April 14, 1912
Wh-what happened?! Where am I?
This staircase is incredible. I must be in a huge mansion somewhere!
But where?
How can they let such riffraff in first class? That boy doesn't belong here.
He should be with the third-class passengers down below.
First class? Third-class passengers down below?
What is this place? Where am I?

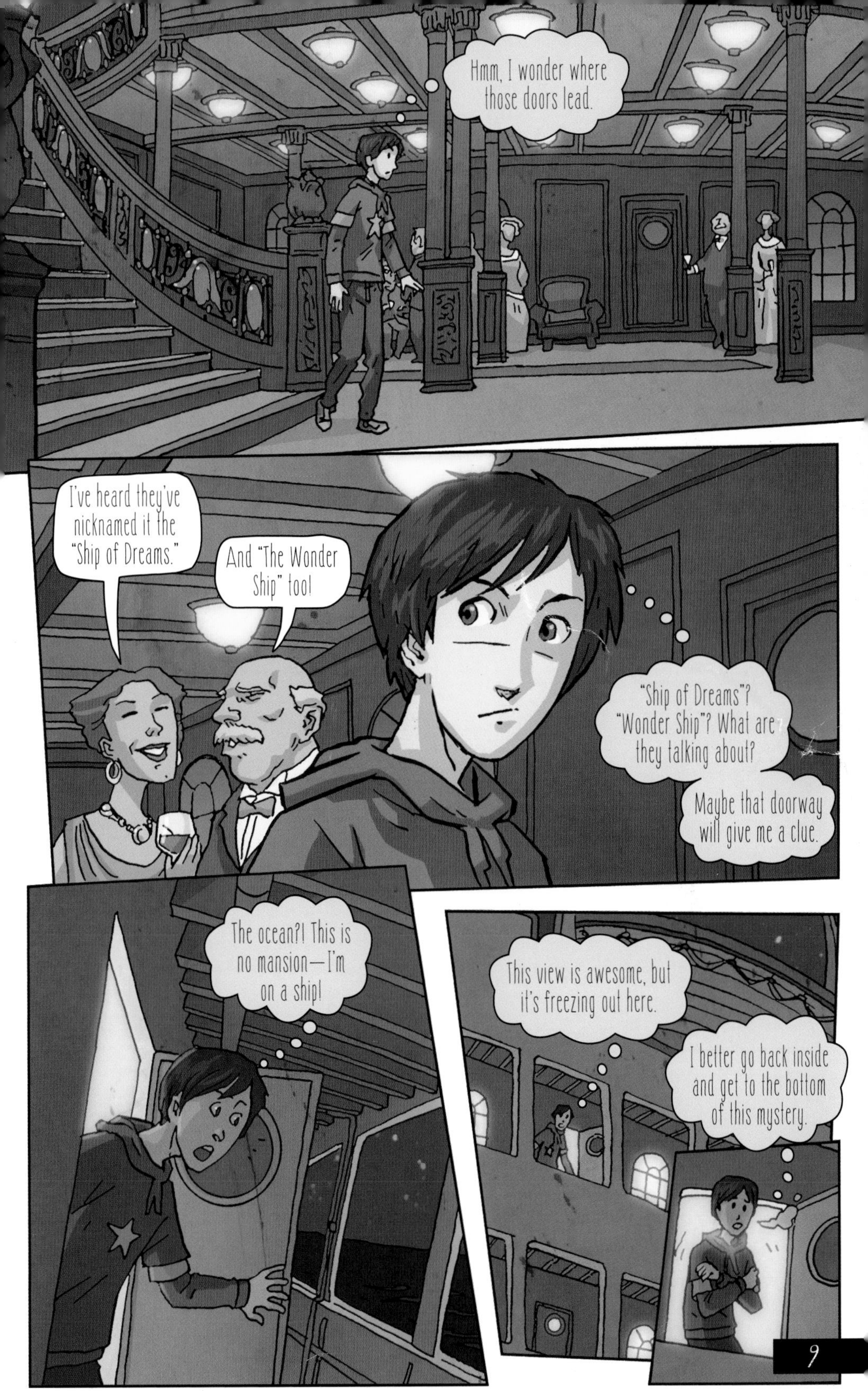
Hmm, I wonder where those doors lead.
I've heard they've nicknamed it the "Ship of Dreams."
And "The Wonder Ship" too!
"Ship of Dreams"? "Wonder Ship"? What are they talking about?
Maybe that doorway will give me a clue.
The ocean?! This is no mansion—I'm on a ship!
This view is awesome, but it's freezing out here.
I better go back inside and get to the bottom of this mystery.

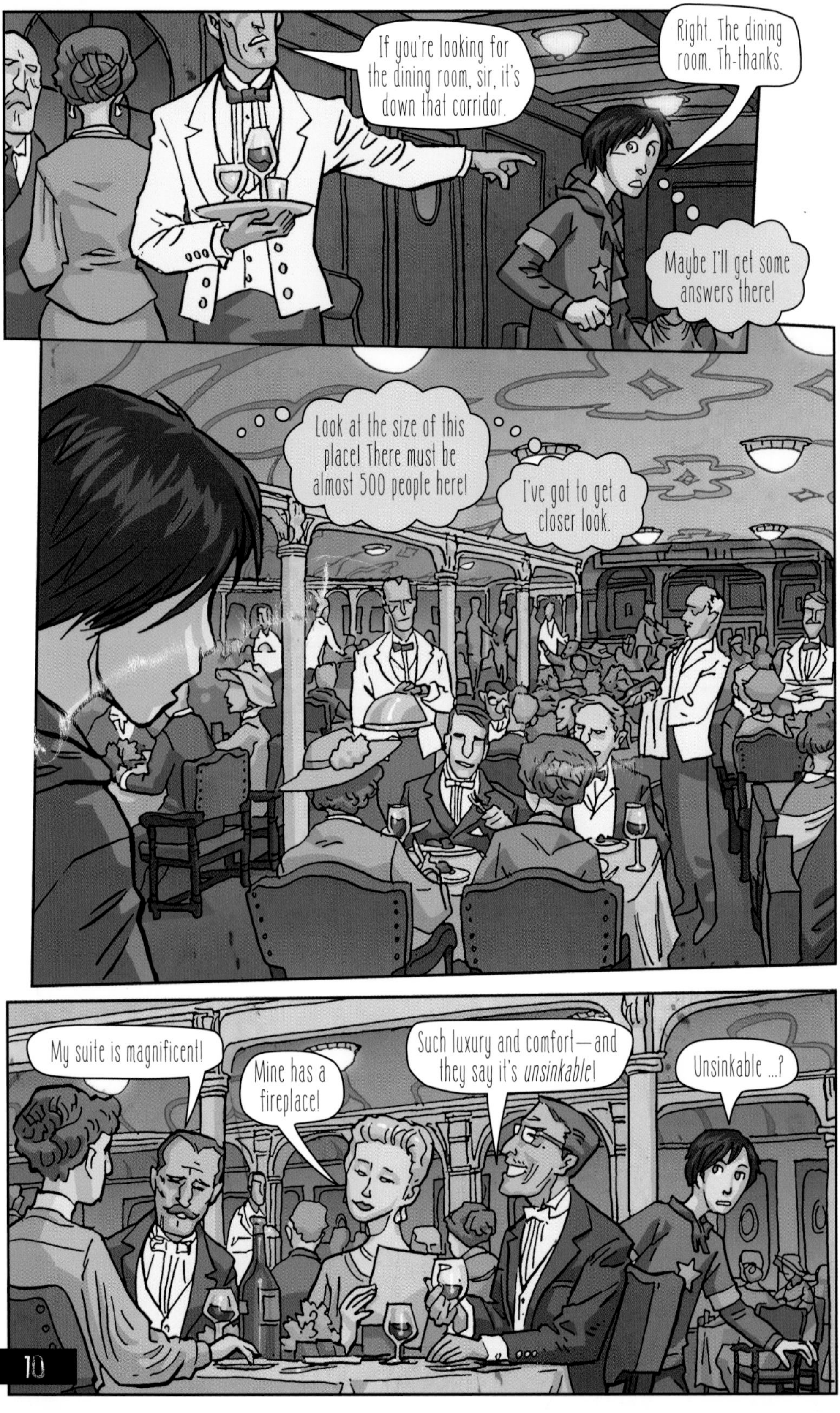
If you're looking for the dining room, sir, it's down that corridor.
Right. The dining room. Th-thanks.
Maybe I'll get some answers there!
Look at the size of this place! There must be almost 500 people here!
I've got to get a closer look.
My suite is magnificent!
Mine has a fireplace!
Such luxury and comfort—and they say it's *unsinkable*!
Unsinkable ...?

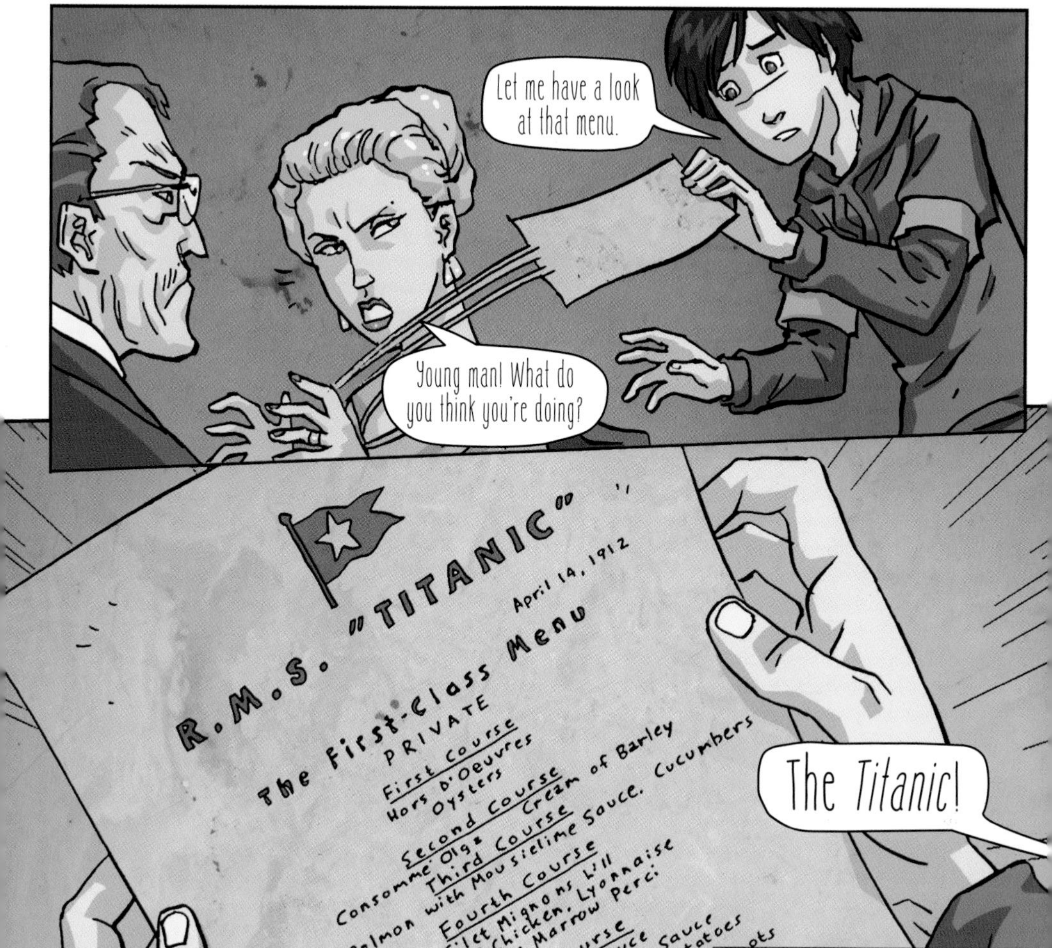
Let me have a look at that menu.
Young man! What do you think you're doing?
R.M.S. "TITANIC"
April 14, 1912
The First-Class Menu
PRIVATE
First Course
Hors D'Oeuvres
Oysters
Second Course
Consomme Olga
Cream of Barley
Third Course
Poached Salmon with Mousieline Sauce. Cucumbers
Fourth Course
Filet Mignons Lili
Saute of Chicken, Lyonnaise
Fifth Course
Lamb, Mint Sauce
Roast Duckling, Apple Sauce
Sirloin of Beef, Chateau Potatoes
Green Pea
Boiled Rice
Sixth Course
Seventh Course
The *Titanic*!
April 14, 1912?!
Oh no! We've got only a few hours to live!

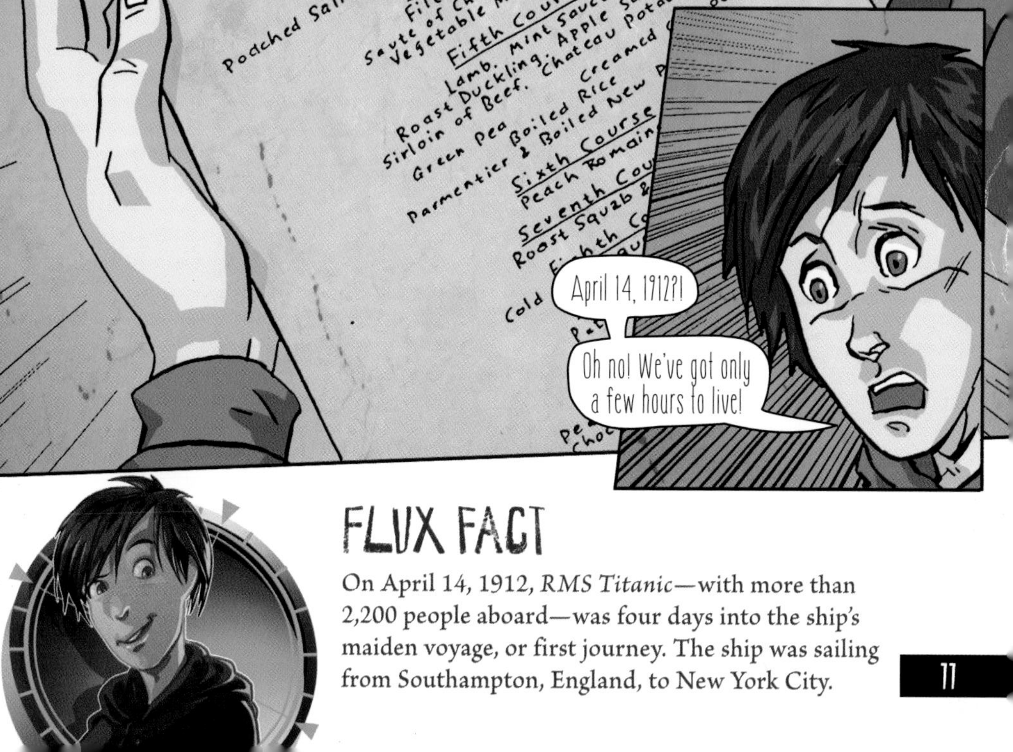

FLUX FACT

On April 14, 1912, *RMS Titanic*—with more than 2,200 people aboard—was four days into the ship's maiden voyage, or first journey. The ship was sailing from Southampton, England, to New York City.

CHAPTER THREE
"ICEBERG RIGHT AHEAD!"

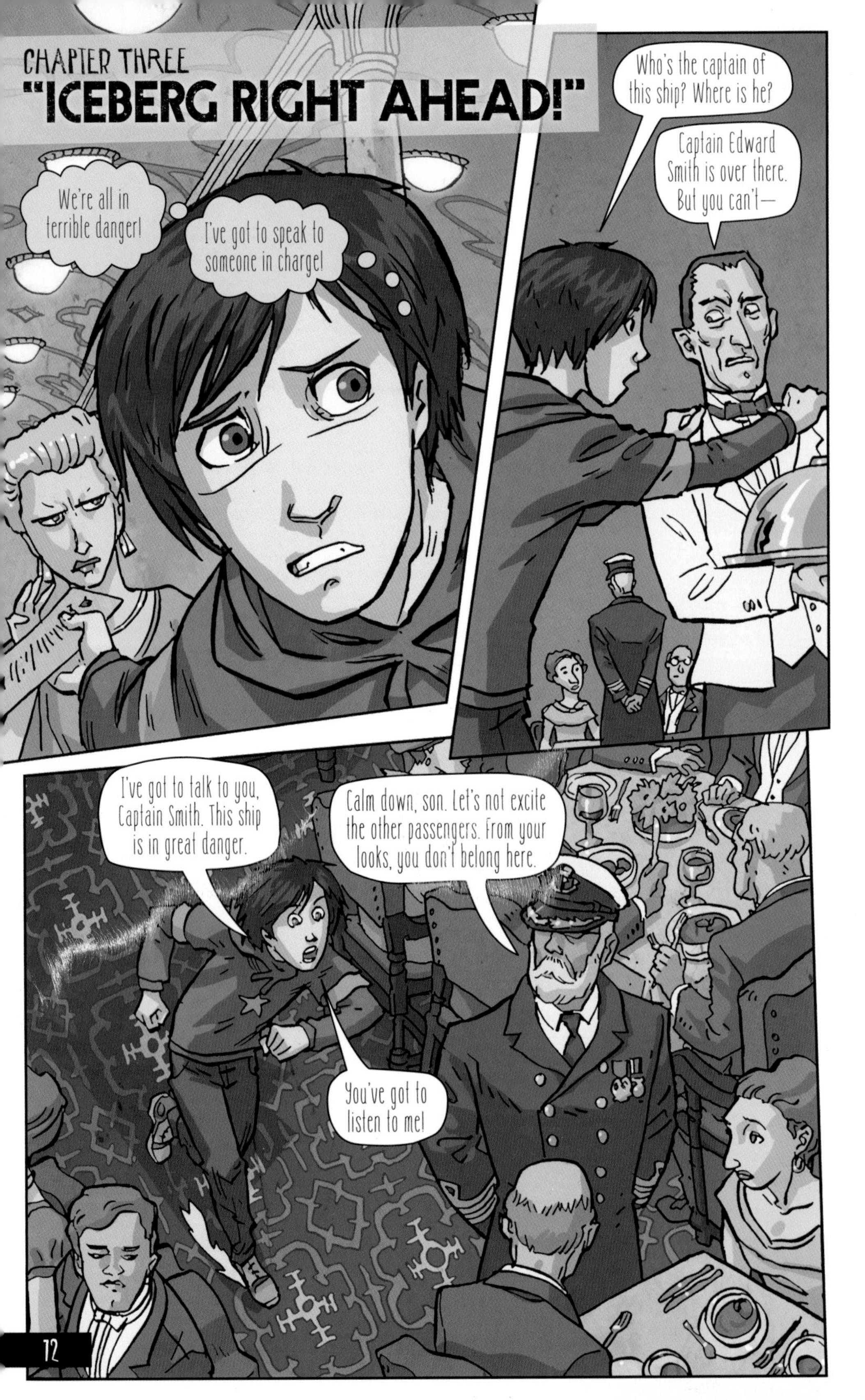
We're all in terrible danger!
I've got to speak to someone in charge!
Who's the captain of this ship? Where is he?
Captain Edward Smith is over there. But you can't—
I've got to talk to you, Captain Smith. This ship is in great danger.
Calm down, son. Let's not excite the other passengers. From your looks, you don't belong here.
You've got to listen to me!

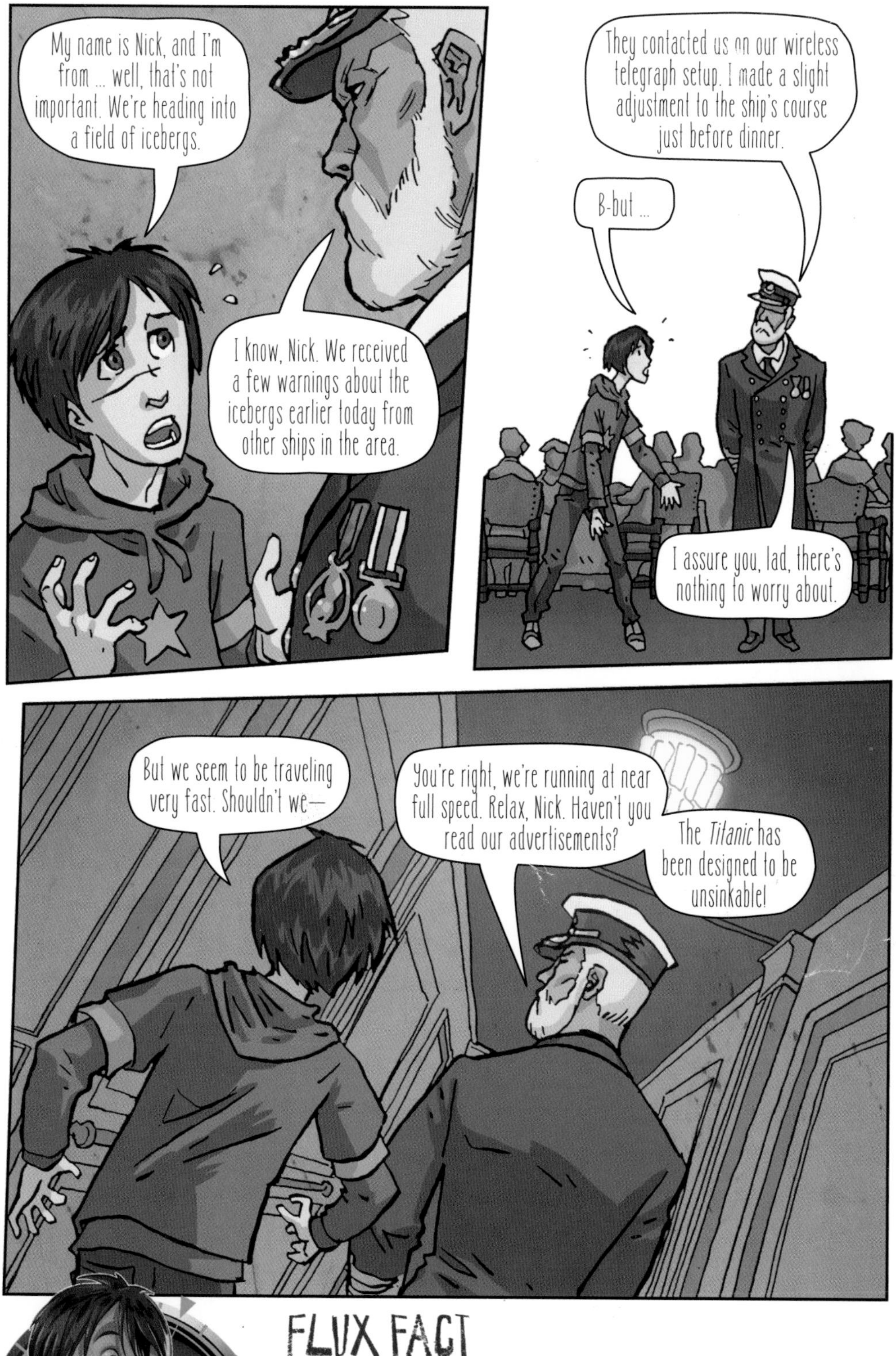
My name is Nick, and I'm from ... well, that's not important. We're heading into a field of icebergs.
I know, Nick. We received a few warnings about the icebergs earlier today from other ships in the area.
They contacted us on our wireless telegraph setup. I made a slight adjustment to the ship's course just before dinner.
B-but ...
I assure you, lad, there's nothing to worry about.
But we seem to be traveling very fast. Shouldn't we—
You're right, we're running at near full speed. Relax, Nick. Haven't you read our advertisements?
The *Titanic* has been designed to be unsinkable!

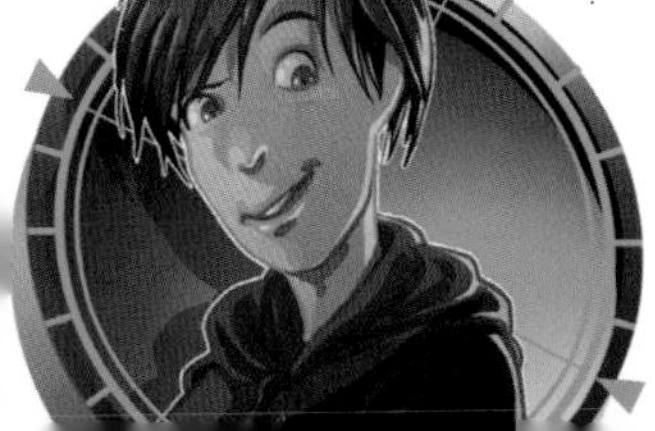

FLUX FACT

Captain Smith was sailing *Titanic* at 22 knots, or 25 miles (40 kilometers) per hour. This was standard sailing procedure, even in icy waters. Smith believed his lookout crew would see ice in plenty of time to avoid it.

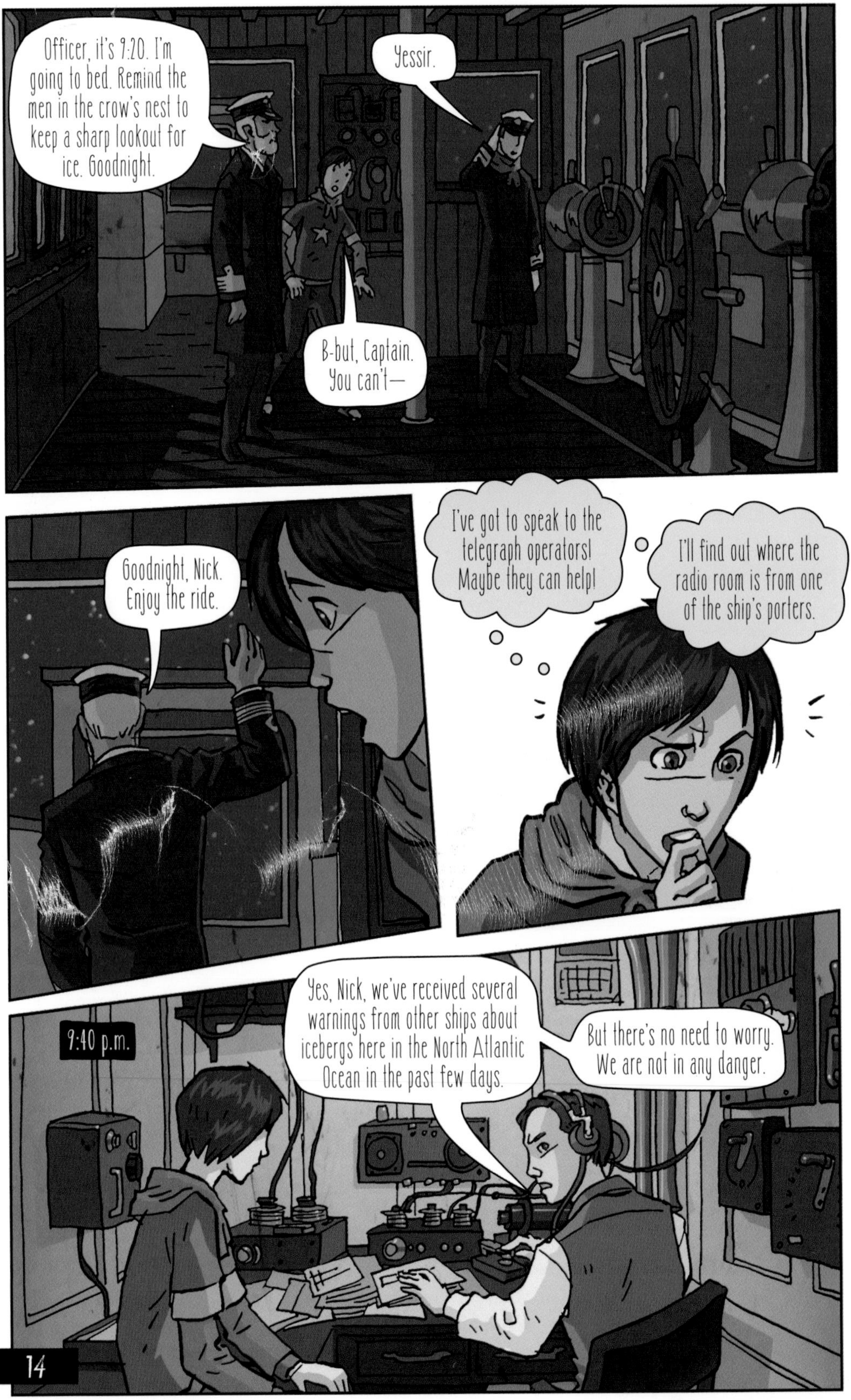
Officer, it's 9:20. I'm going to bed. Remind the men in the crow's nest to keep a sharp lookout for ice. Goodnight.
Yessir.
B-but, Captain. You can't—
Goodnight, Nick. Enjoy the ride.
I've got to speak to the telegraph operators! Maybe they can help!
I'll find out where the radio room is from one of the ship's porters.
9:40 p.m.
Yes, Nick, we've received several warnings from other ships about icebergs here in the North Atlantic Ocean in the past few days.
But there's no need to worry. We are not in any danger.

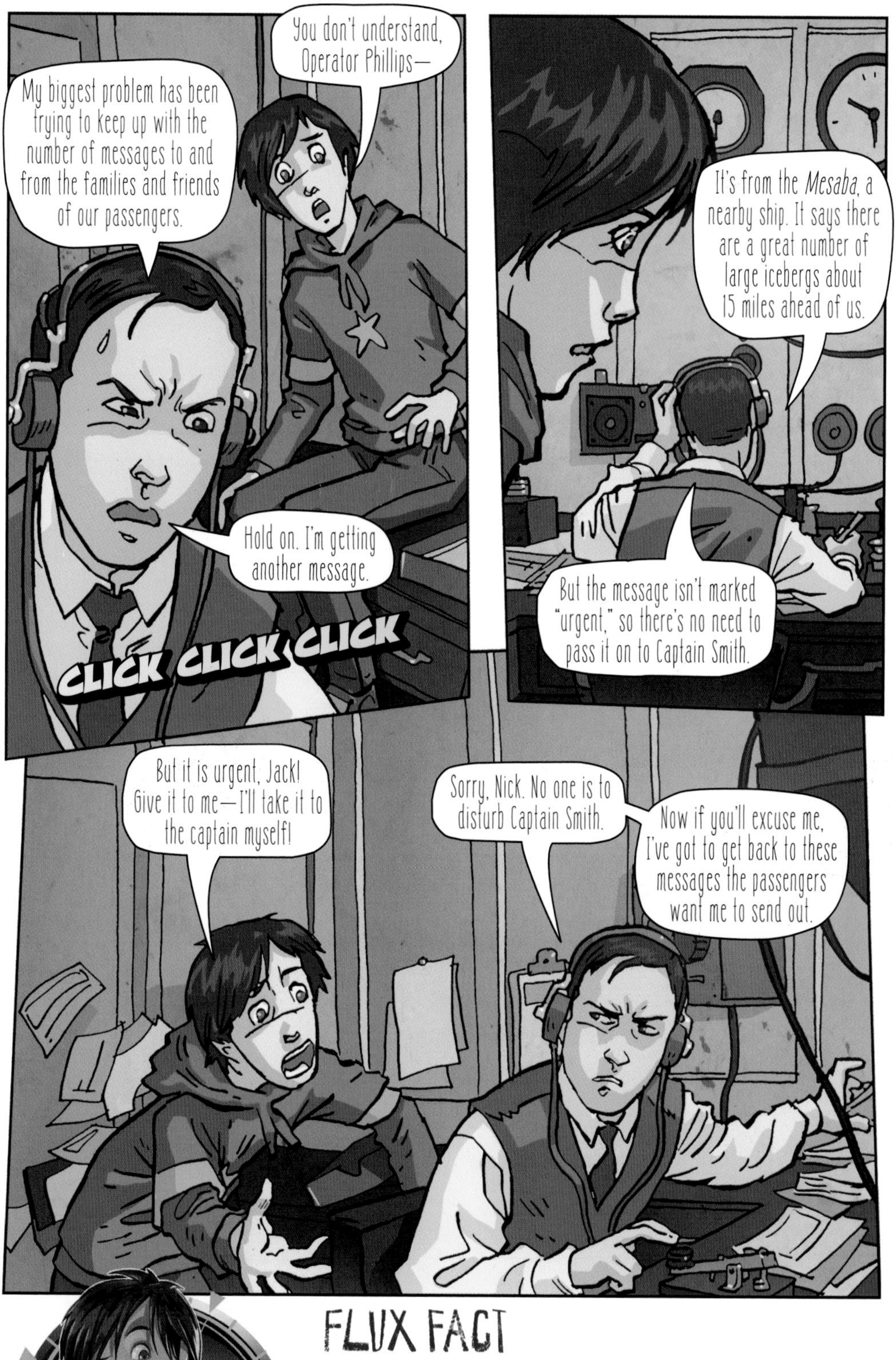
My biggest problem has been trying to keep up with the number of messages to and from the families and friends of our passengers.
You don't understand, Operator Phillips—
Hold on. I'm getting another message.
CLICK CLICK CLICK
It's from the *Mesaba*, a nearby ship. It says there are a great number of large icebergs about 15 miles ahead of us.
But the message isn't marked "urgent," so there's no need to pass it on to Captain Smith.
But it is urgent, Jack! Give it to me—I'll take it to the captain myself!
Sorry, Nick. No one is to disturb Captain Smith.
Now if you'll excuse me, I've got to get back to these messages the passengers want me to send out.

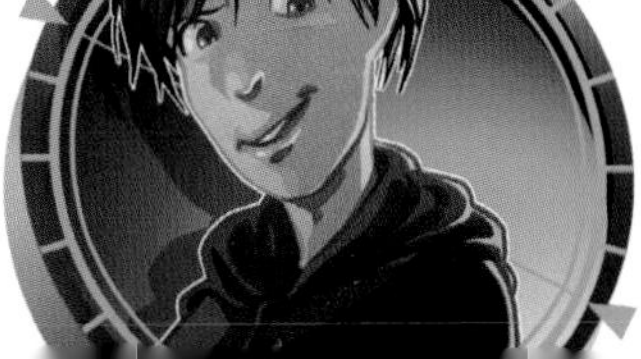

FLUX FACT

The *Titanic*'s new wireless equipment sent Morse code messages to a station in Canada. From there they could be sent to stations in the eastern United States and beyond.

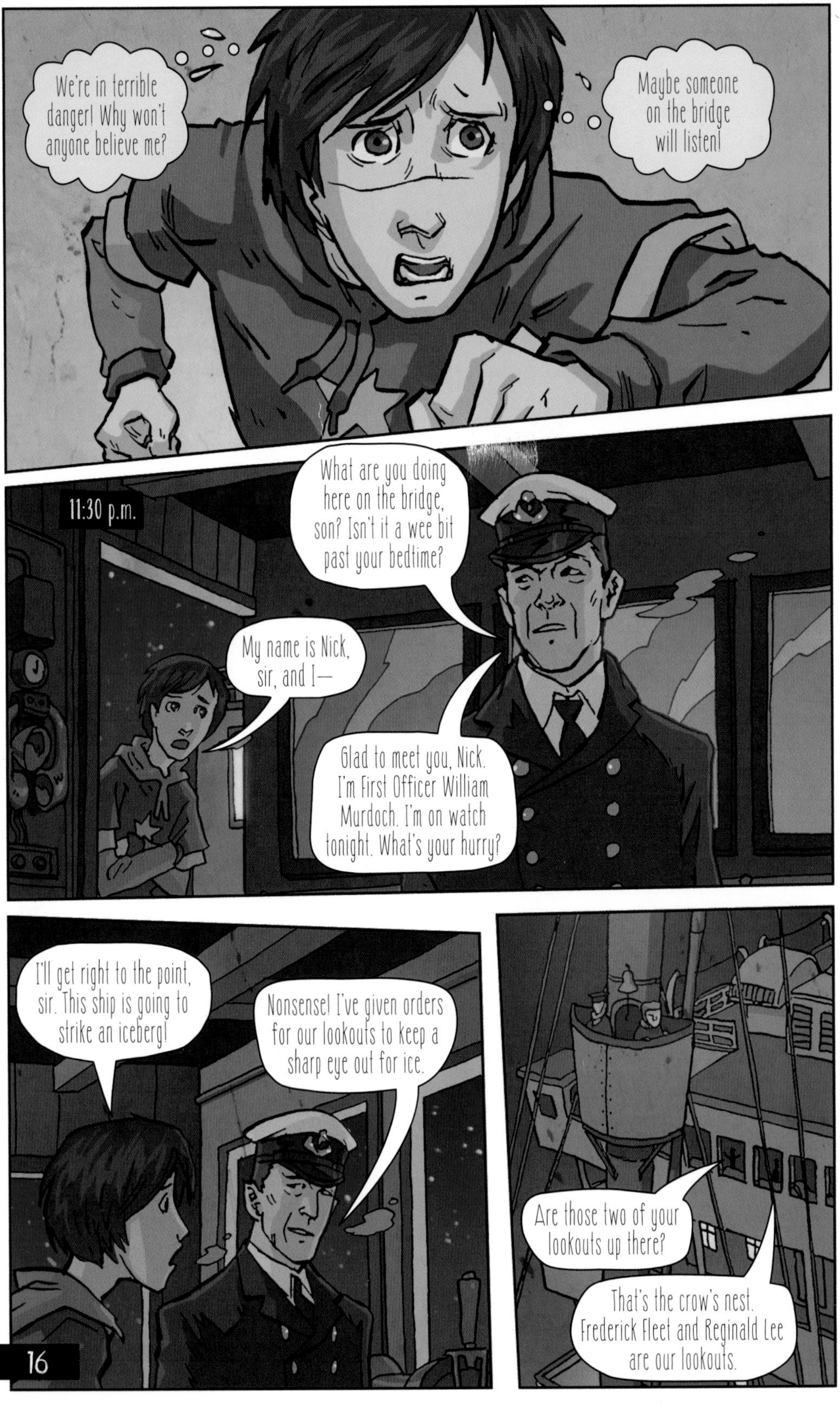
We're in terrible danger! Why won't anyone believe me?
Maybe someone on the bridge will listen!
11:30 p.m.
What are you doing here on the bridge, son? Isn't it a wee bit past your bedtime?
My name is Nick, sir, and I—
Glad to meet you, Nick. I'm First Officer William Murdoch. I'm on watch tonight. What's your hurry?
I'll get right to the point, sir. This ship is going to strike an iceberg!
Nonsense! I've given orders for our lookouts to keep a sharp eye out for ice.
Are those two of your lookouts up there?
That's the crow's nest. Frederick Fleet and Reginald Lee are our lookouts.

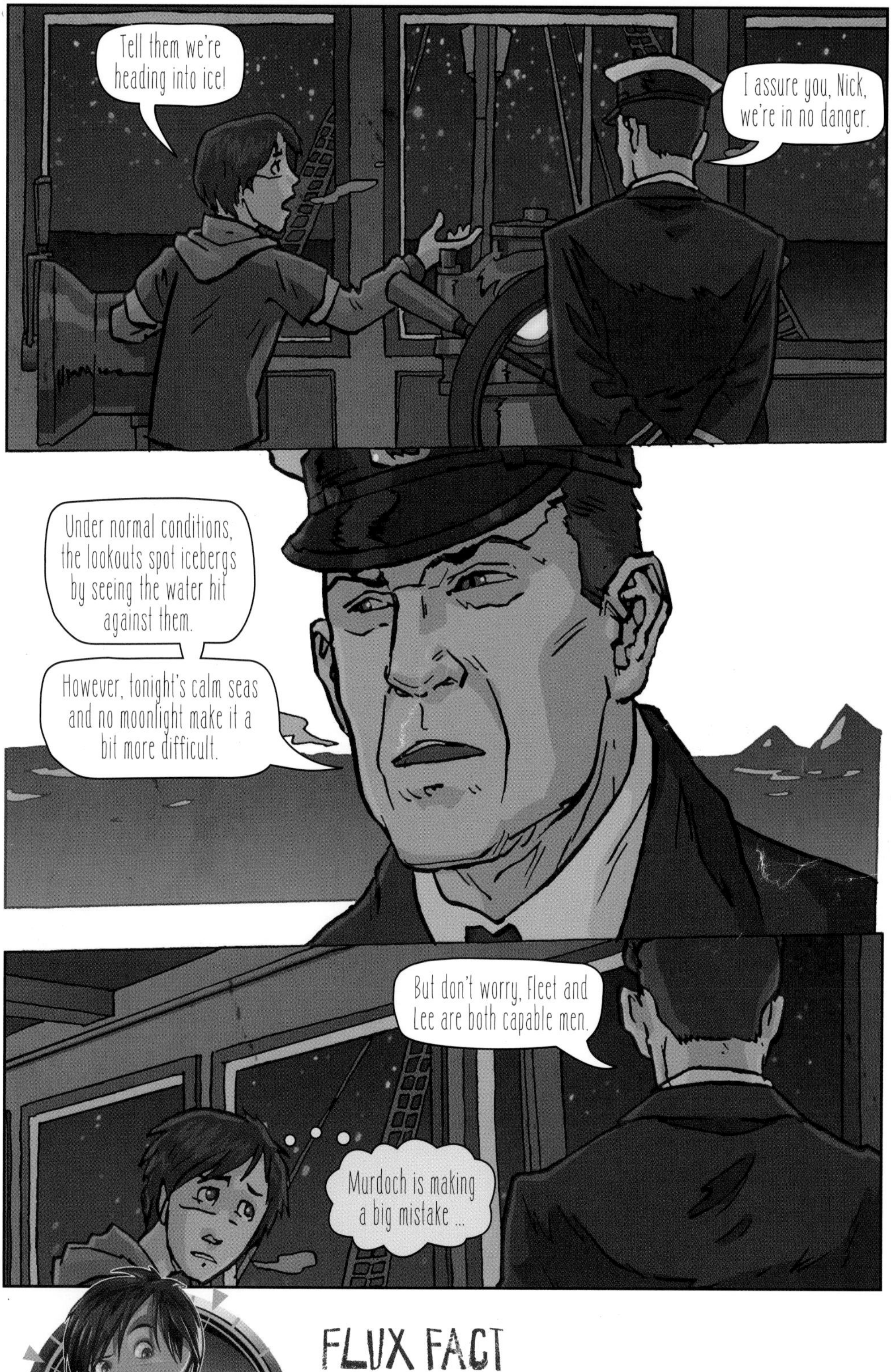
Tell them we're heading into ice!
I assure you, Nick, we're in no danger.
Under normal conditions, the lookouts spot icebergs by seeing the water hit against them.
However, tonight's calm seas and no moonlight make it a bit more difficult.
But don't worry, Fleet and Lee are both capable men.
Murdoch is making a big mistake ...

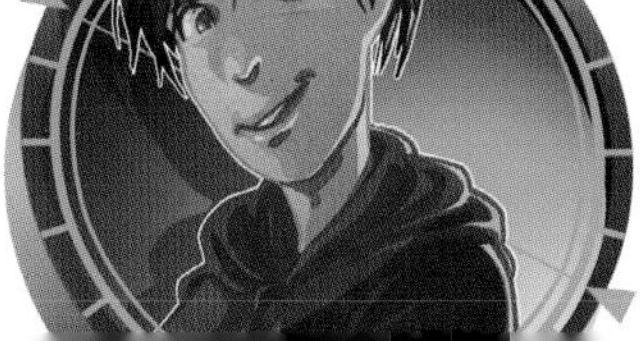

FLUX FACT

The maiden voyage of the *Titanic* was the fifth maiden voyage First Officer William Murdoch took part in. It would be his last.

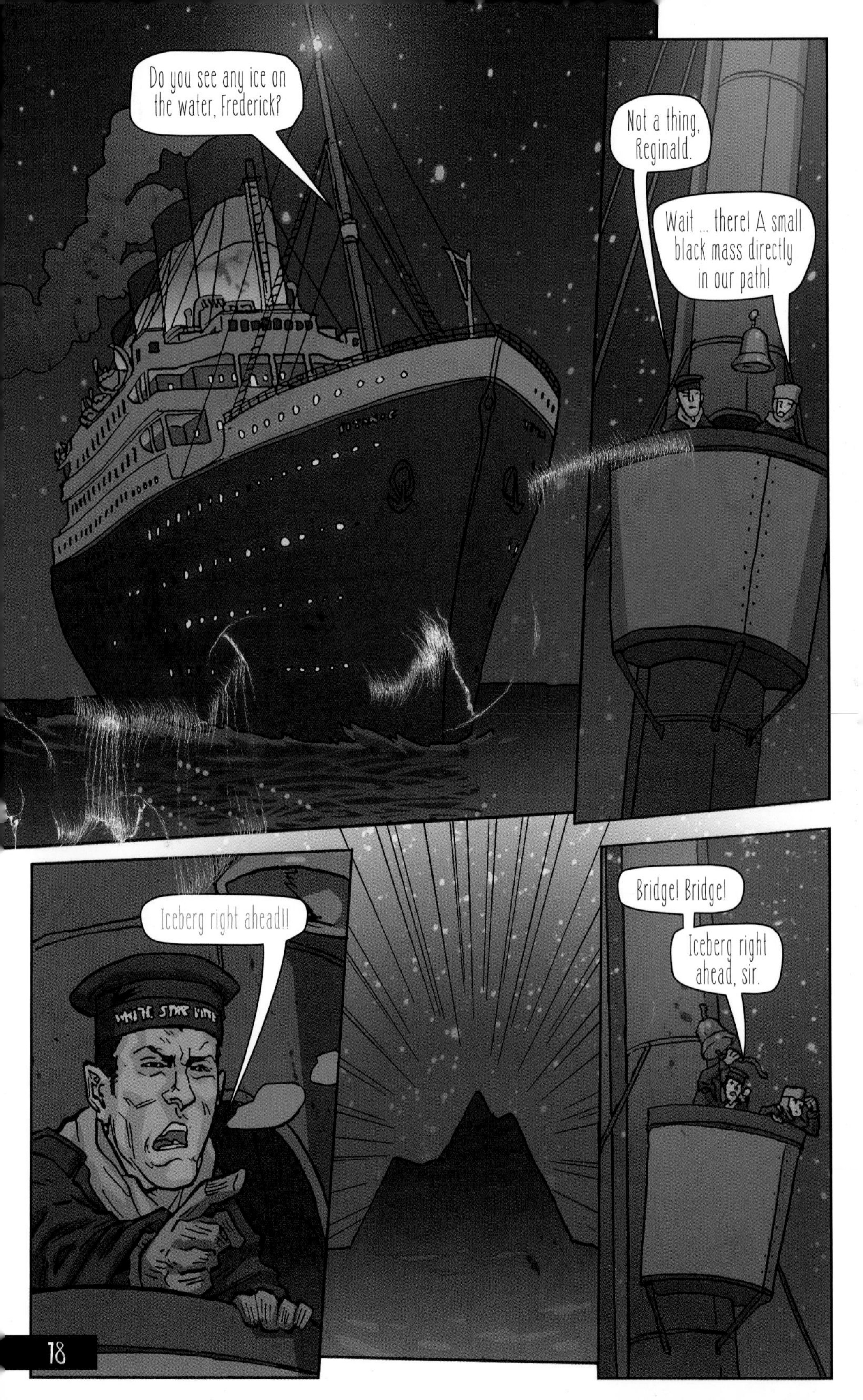
Do you see any ice on the water, Frederick?
Not a thing, Reginald.
Wait ... there! A small black mass directly in our path!
Iceberg right ahead!!
Bridge! Bridge!
Iceberg right ahead, sir.

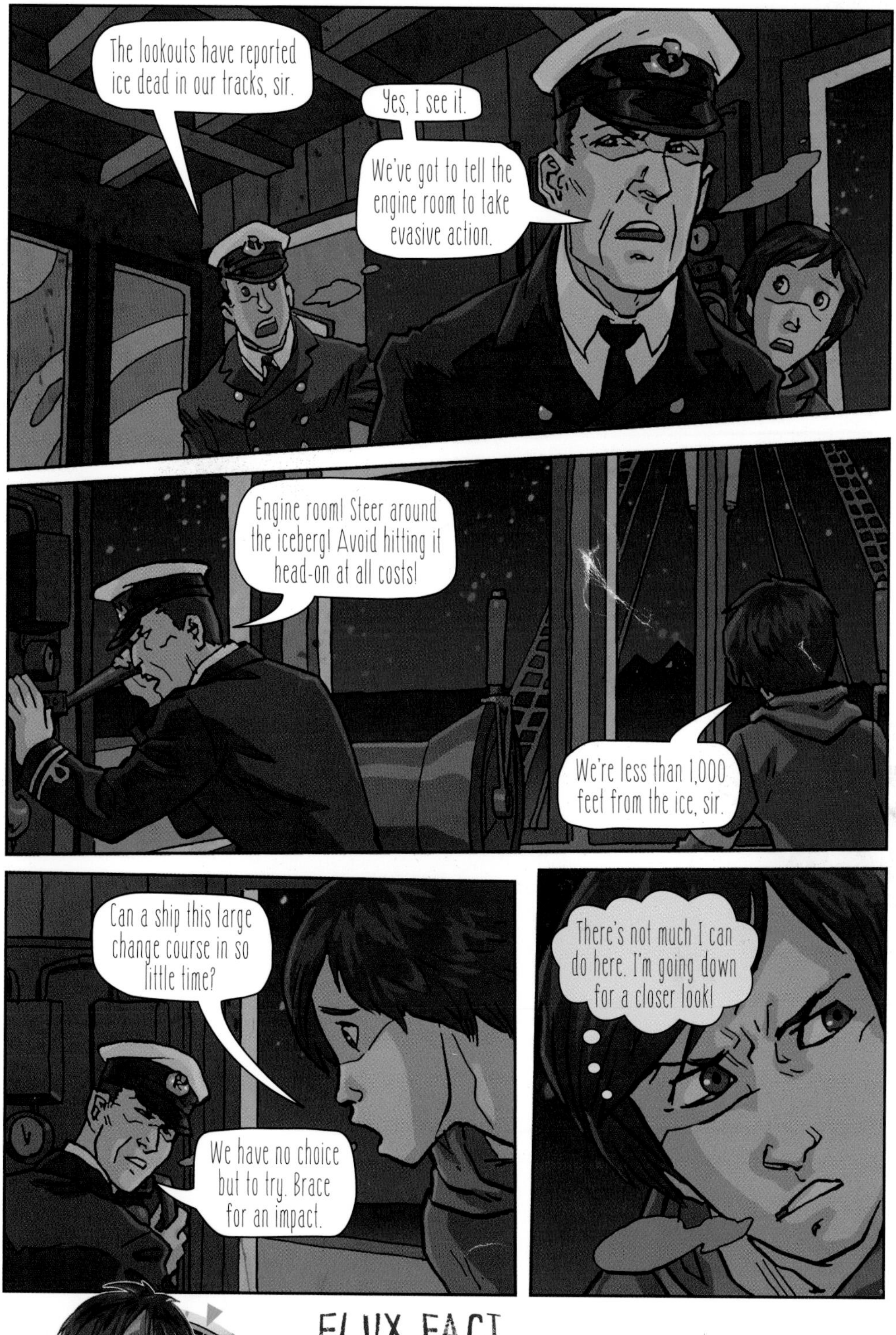
The lookouts have reported ice dead in our tracks, sir.
Yes, I see it.
We've got to tell the engine room to take evasive action.
Engine room! Steer around the iceberg! Avoid hitting it head-on at all costs!
We're less than 1,000 feet from the ice, sir.
Can a ship this large change course in so little time?
We have no choice but to try. Brace for an impact.
There's not much I can do here. I'm going down for a closer look!

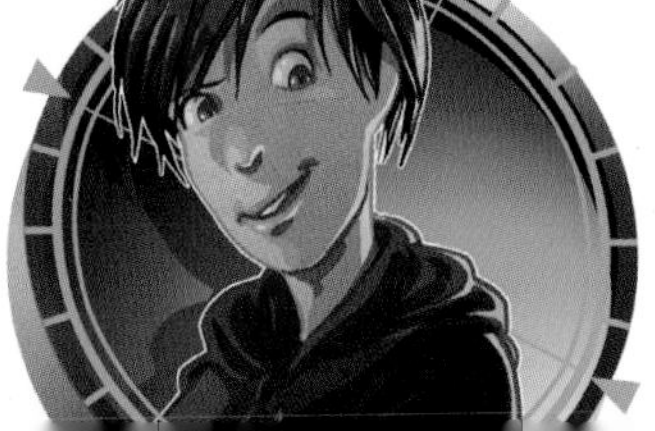

FLUX FACT

Frederick Fleet would have seen the iceberg sooner—if he had binoculars. The lookouts were issued binoculars at the beginning of the voyage, but they were taken back and given to crewmen on the bridge.

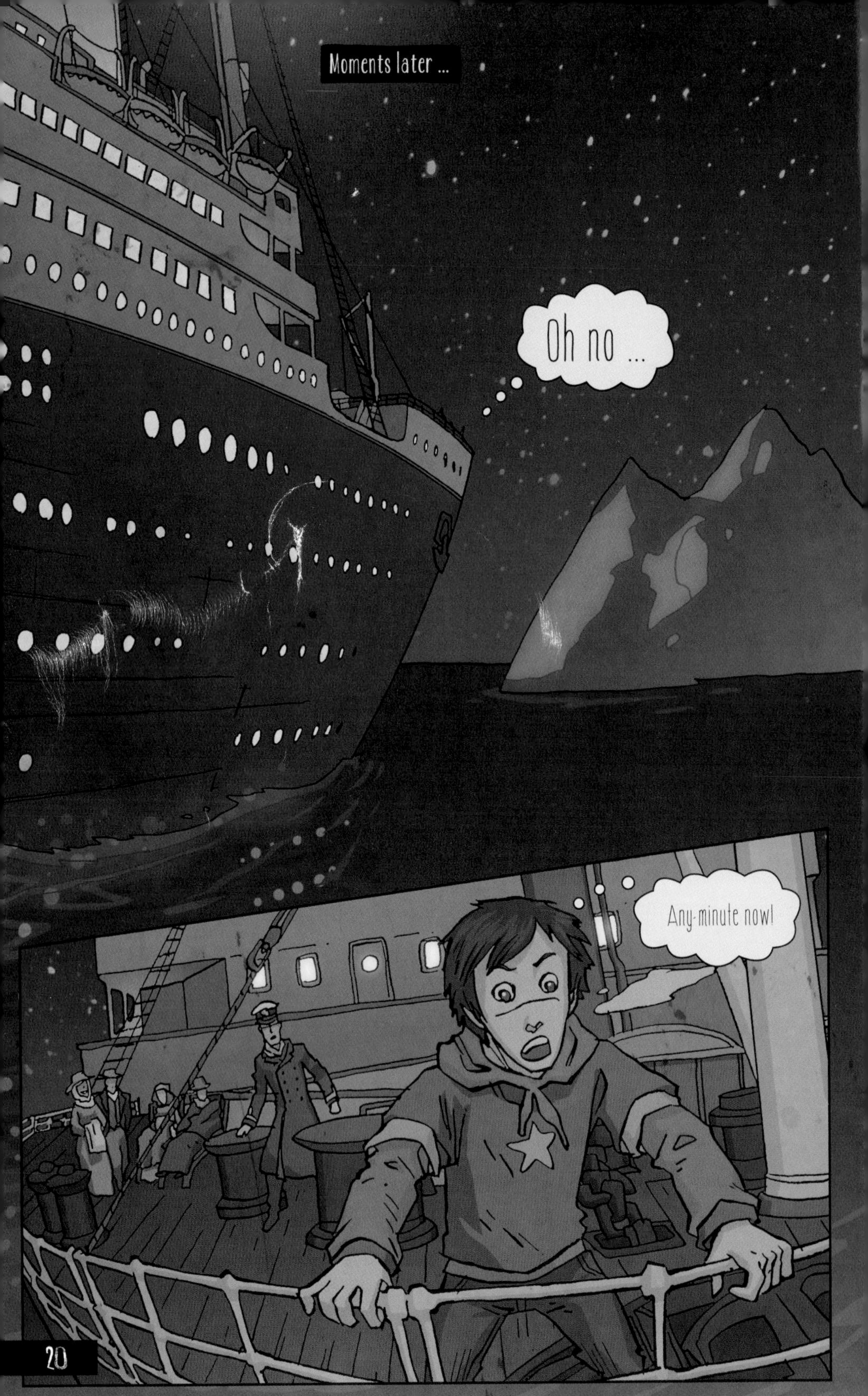
Moments later ...
Oh no ...
Any-minute now!

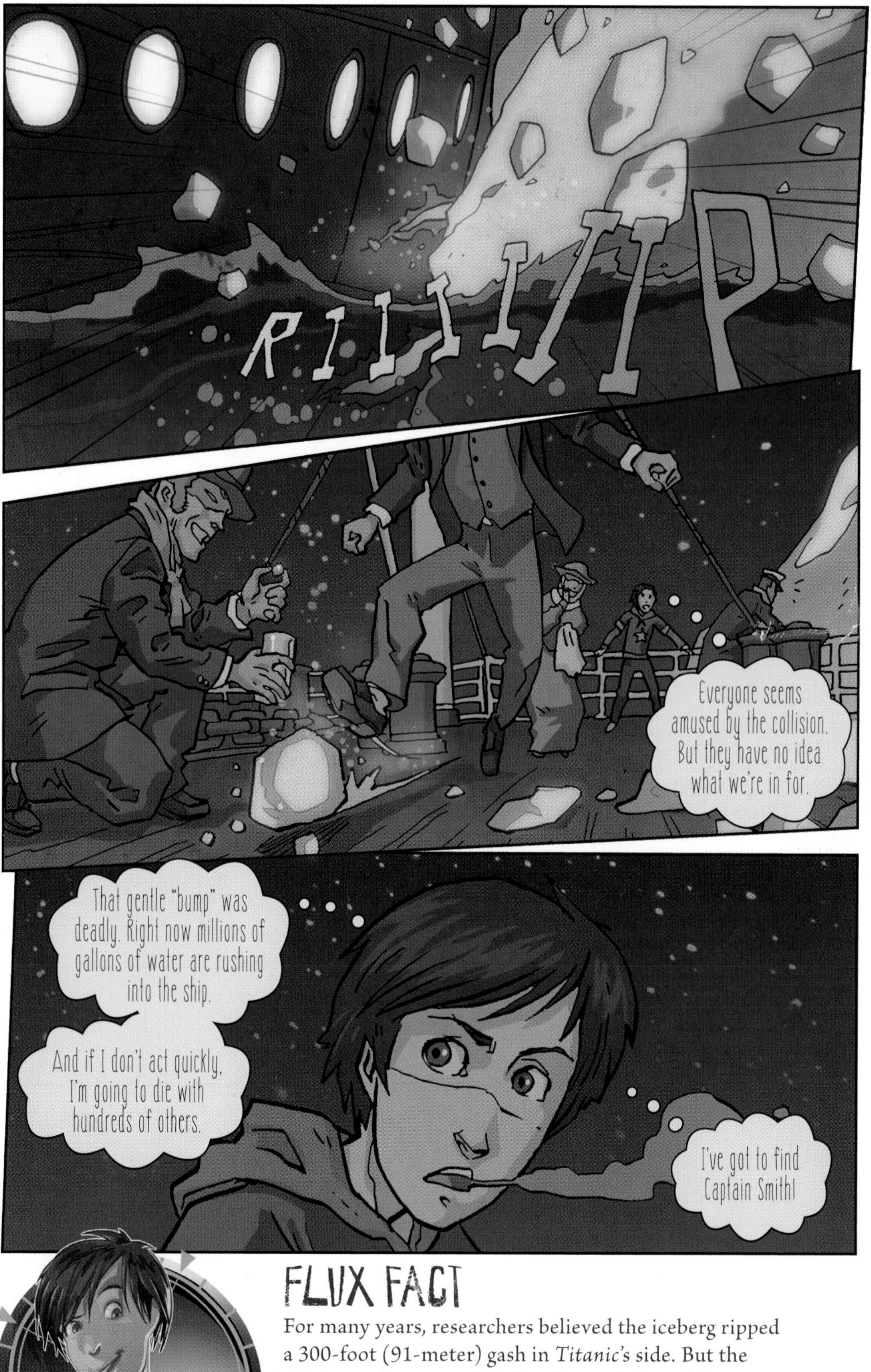
RIIIIIP
Everyone seems amused by the collision. But they have no idea what we're in for.
That gentle "bump" was deadly. Right now millions of gallons of water are rushing into the ship.
And if I don't act quickly, I'm going to die with hundreds of others.
I've got to find Captain Smith!

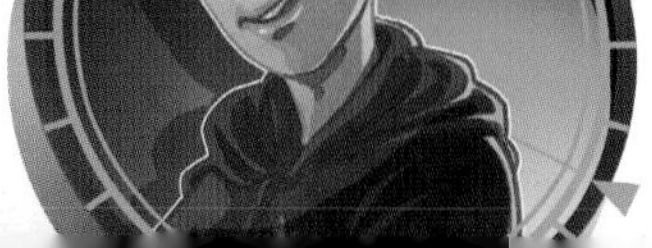

FLUX FACT

For many years, researchers believed the iceberg ripped a 300-foot (91-meter) gash in *Titanic*'s side. But the ship's wreckage revealed that the total area of damage was only about 13 square feet (1.2 square meters).

CHAPTER FOUR

"EVERY MAN FOR HIMSELF"

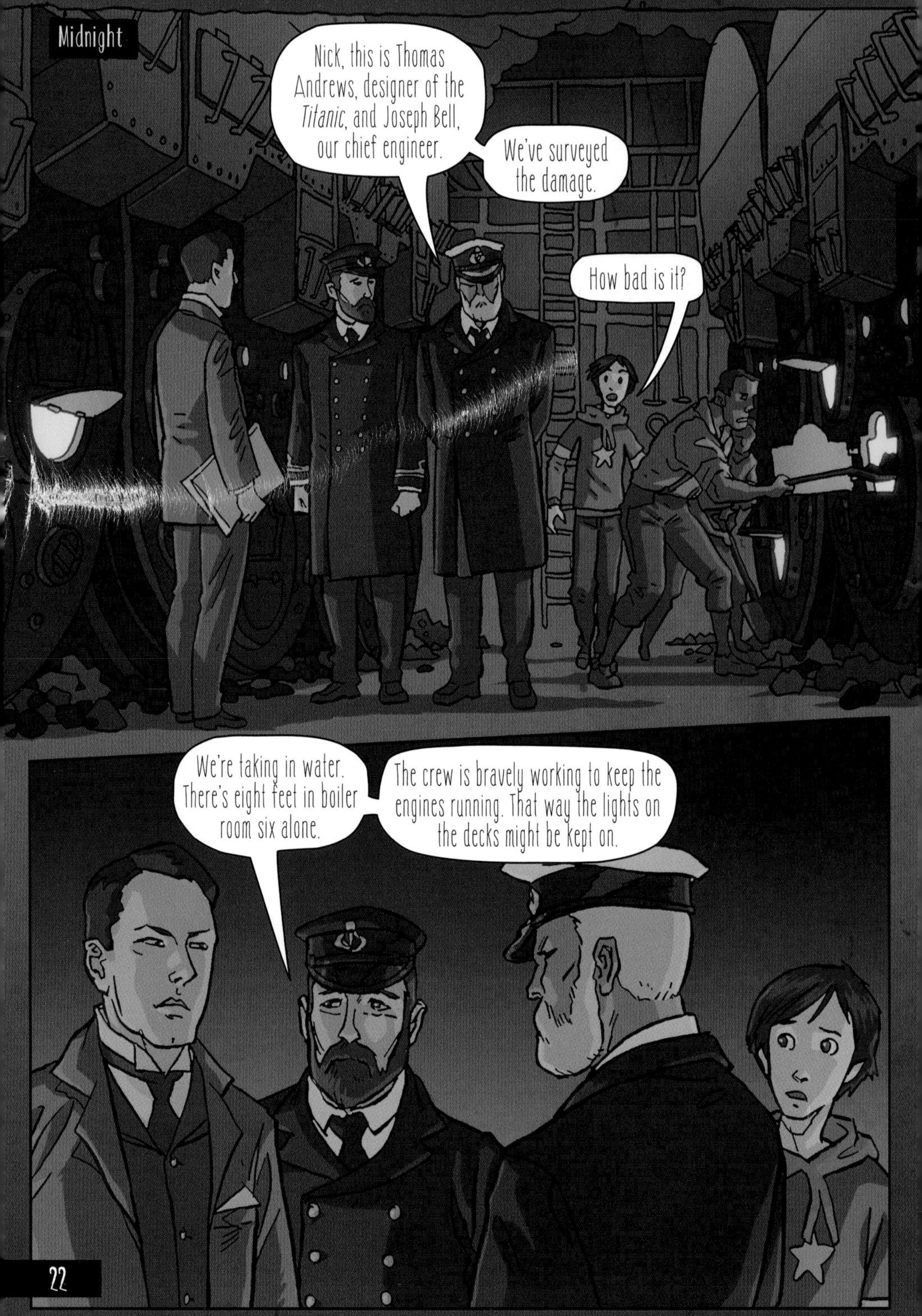

Midnight
Nick, this is Thomas Andrews, designer of the *Titanic*, and Joseph Bell, our chief engineer.
We've surveyed the damage.
How bad is it?
We're taking in water. There's eight feet in boiler room six alone.
The crew is bravely working to keep the engines running. That way the lights on the decks might be kept on.

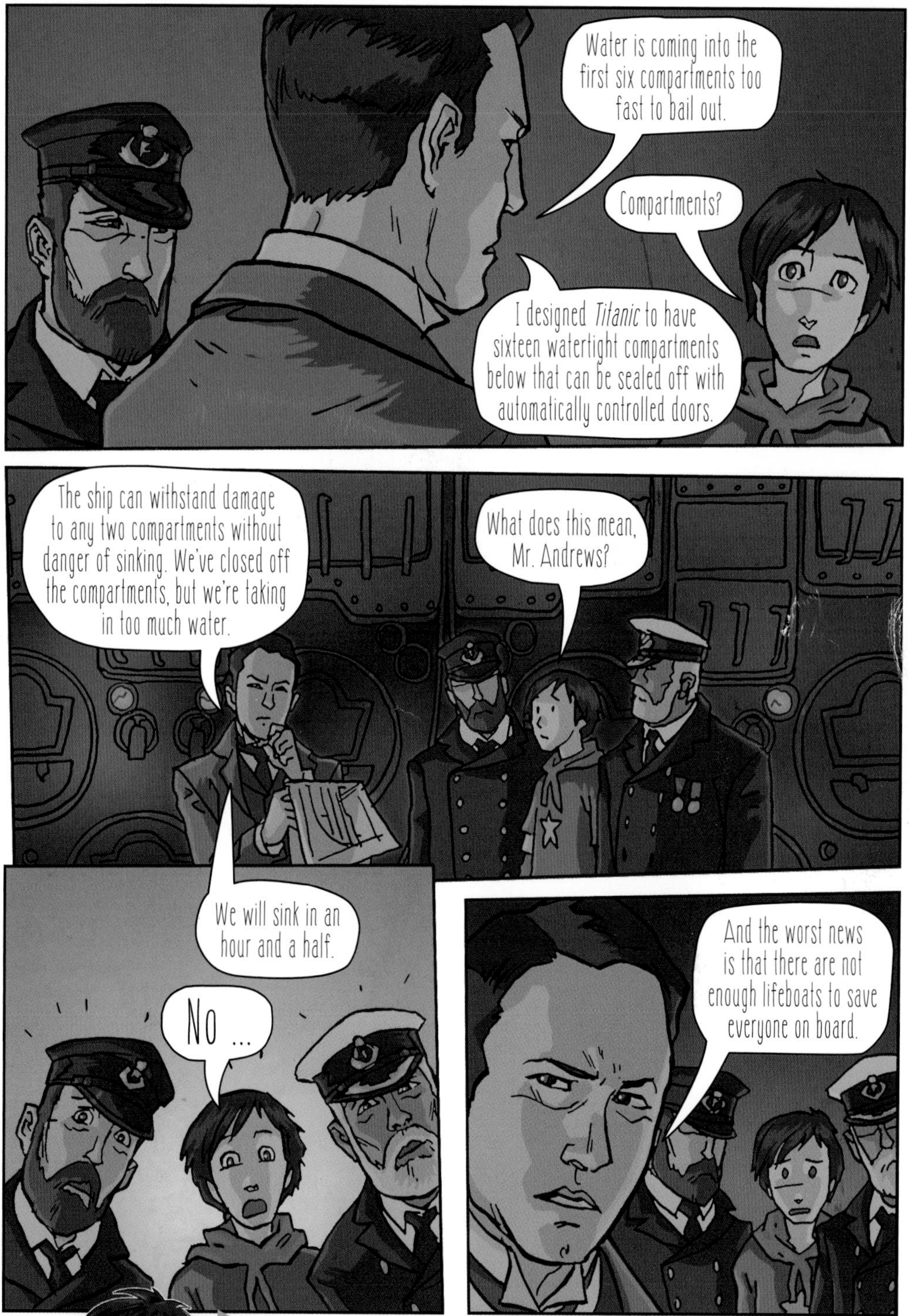
Water is coming into the first six compartments too fast to bail out.
Compartments?
I designed Titanic to have sixteen watertight compartments below that can be sealed off with automatically controlled doors.
The ship can withstand damage to any two compartments without danger of sinking. We've closed off the compartments, but we're taking in too much water.
What does this mean, Mr. Andrews?
We will sink in an hour and a half.
No ...
And the worst news is that there are not enough lifeboats to save everyone on board.

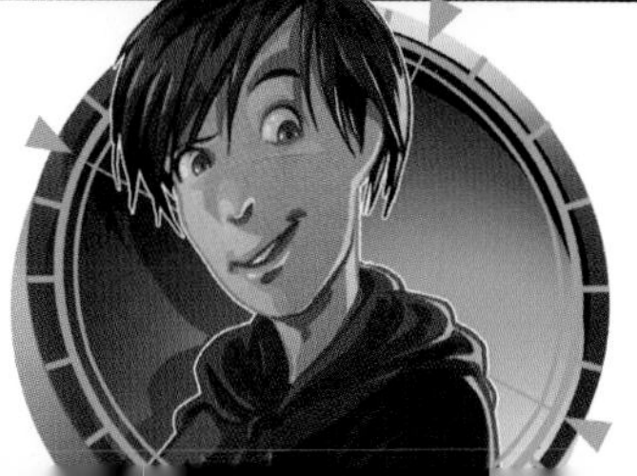

FLUX FACT

After the collision, the *Titanic* sent a telegraph message to the nearby *Californian* asking for help. But the operator had gone to bed. The *Californian* could have saved hundreds of lives.

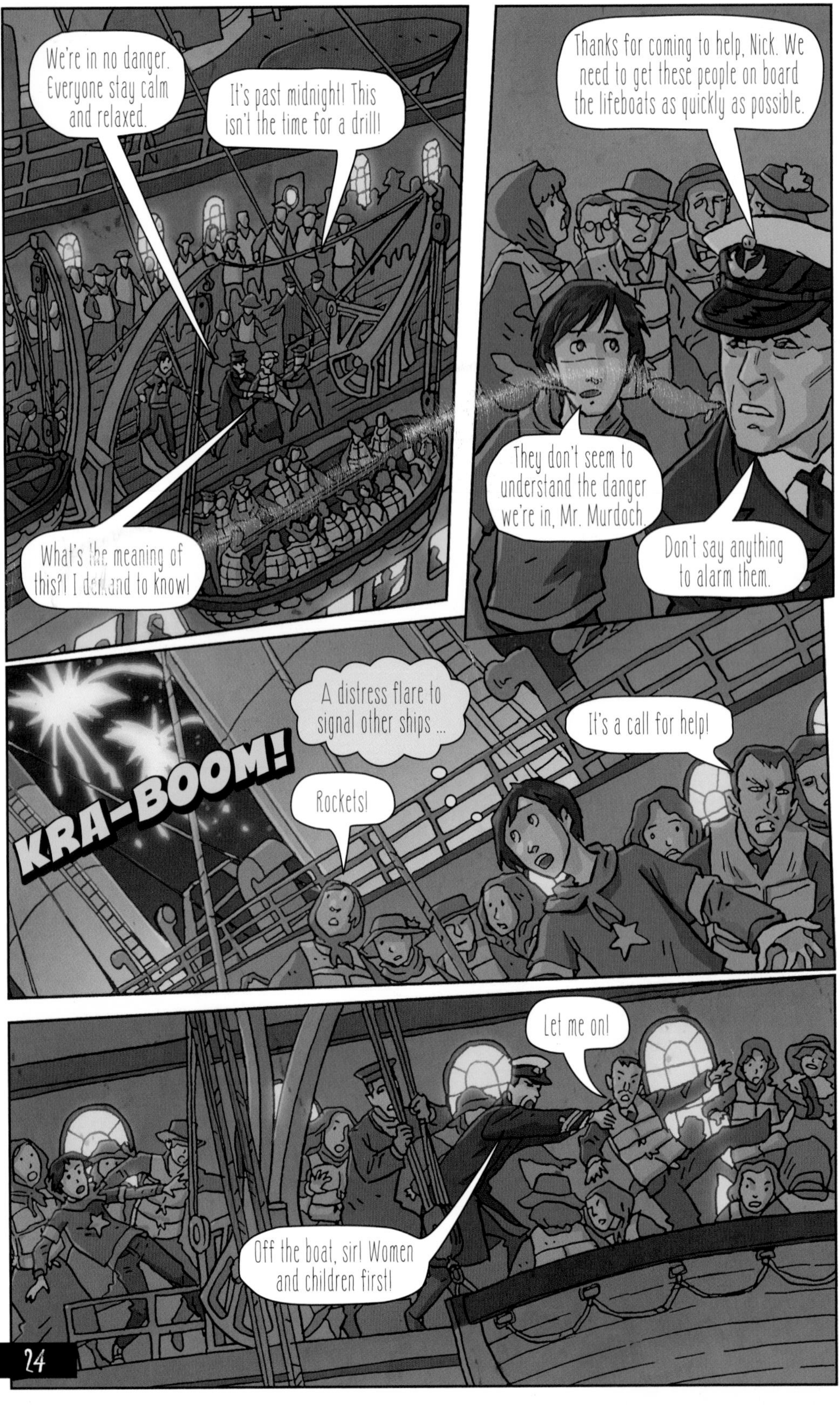
We're in no danger. Everyone stay calm and relaxed.
It's past midnight! This isn't the time for a drill!
What's the meaning of this?! I demand to know!
Thanks for coming to help, Nick. We need to get these people on board the lifeboats as quickly as possible.
They don't seem to understand the danger we're in, Mr. Murdoch.
Don't say anything to alarm them.
KRA-BOOM!
Rockets!
A distress flare to signal other ships ...
It's a call for help!
Let me on!
Off the boat, sir! Women and children first!

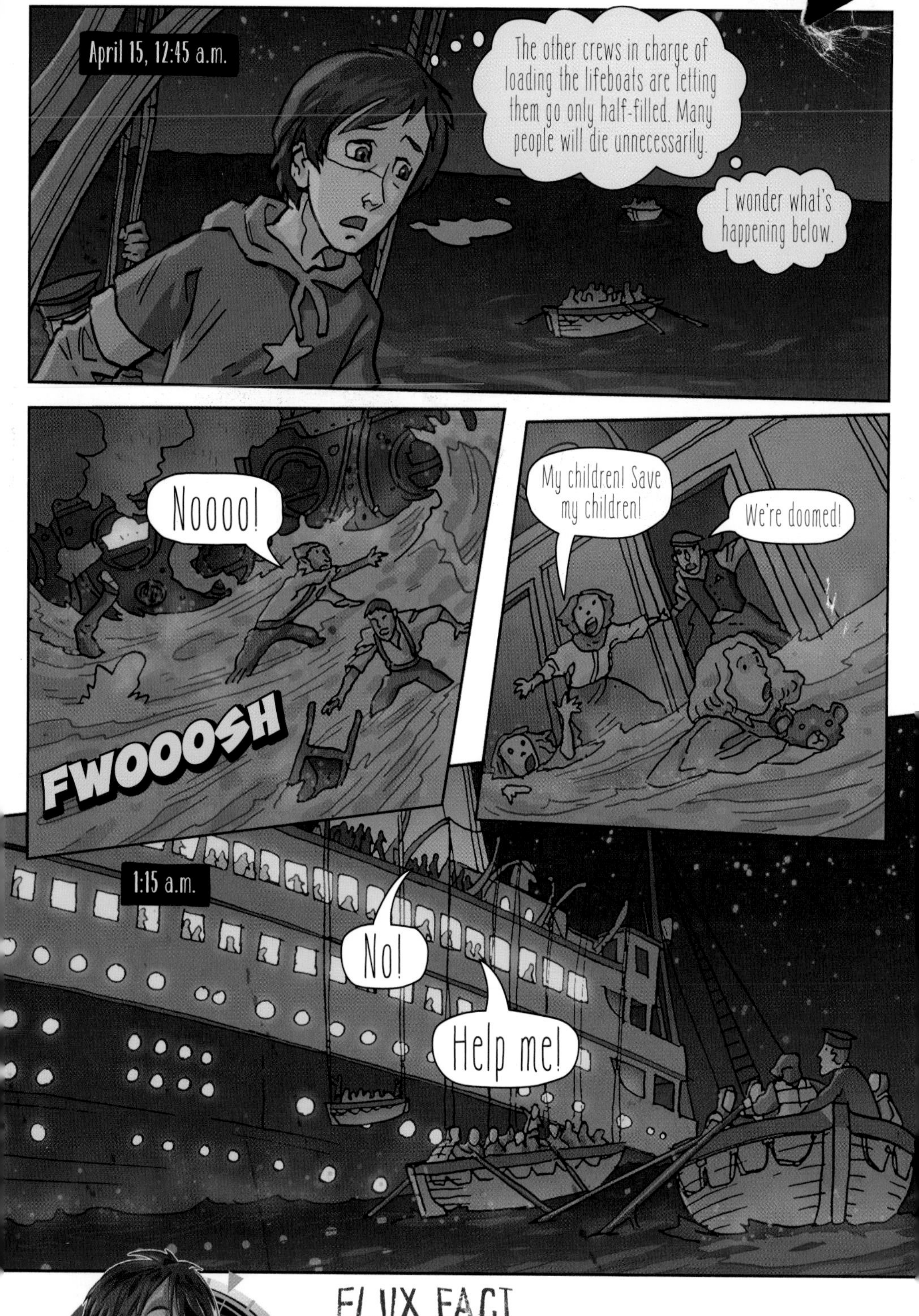
April 15, 12:45 a.m.
The other crews in charge of loading the lifeboats are letting them go only half-filled. Many people will die unnecessarily.
I wonder what's happening below.
Noooo!
FWOOOSH
My children! Save my children!
We're doomed!
1:15 a.m.
No!
Help me!

FLUX FACT

To preserve a better view of the open seas from the top deck, only 16 lifeboats and 4 small rafts were installed on the *Titanic*. Still, the number of lifeboats met the safety requirements of the time.

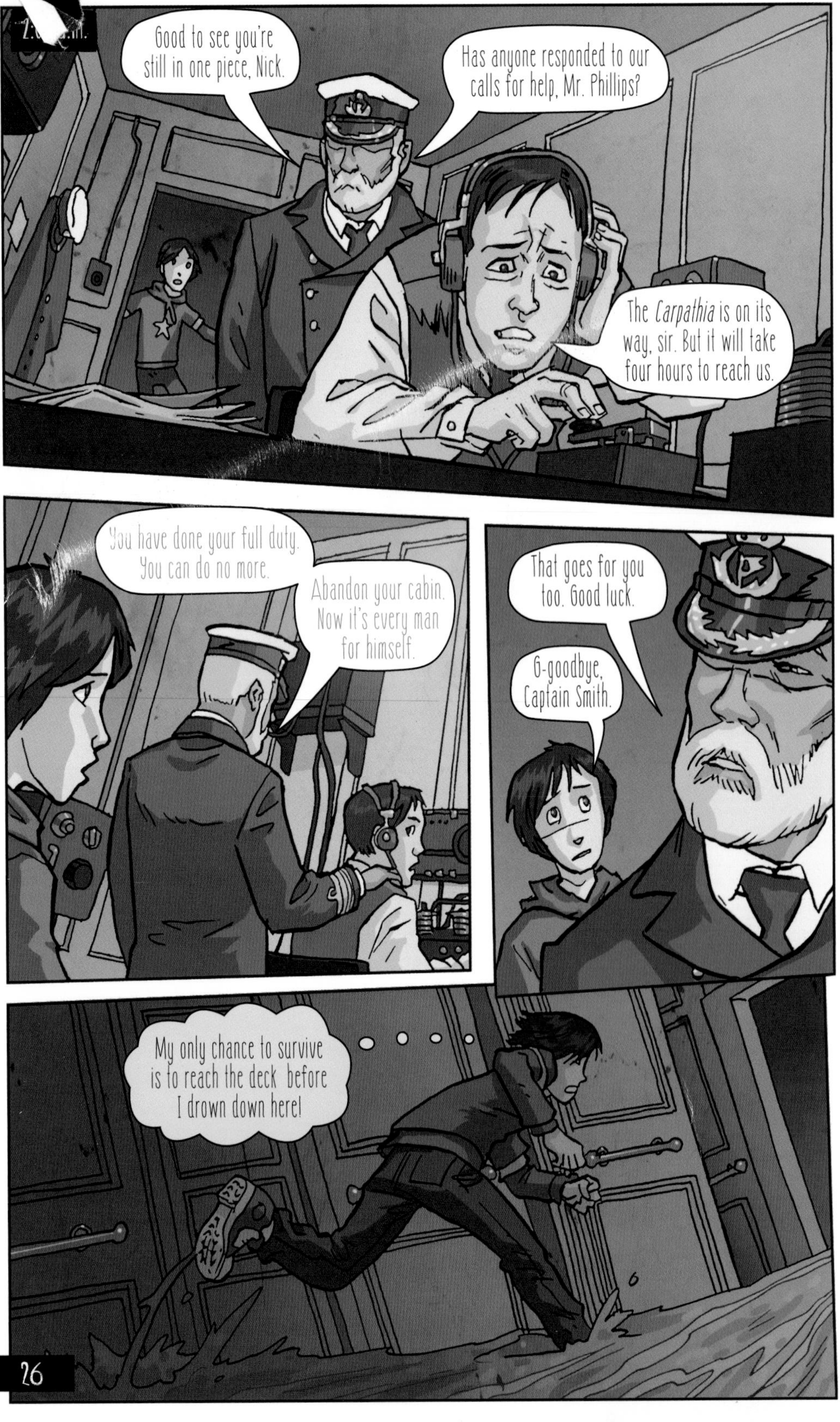
Good to see you're still in one piece, Nick.
Has anyone responded to our calls for help, Mr. Phillips?
The *Carpathia* is on its way, sir. But it will take four hours to reach us.
You have done your full duty. You can do no more.
Abandon your cabin. Now it's every man for himself.
That goes for you too. Good luck.
G-goodbye, Captain Smith.
My only chance to survive is to reach the deck before I drown down here!

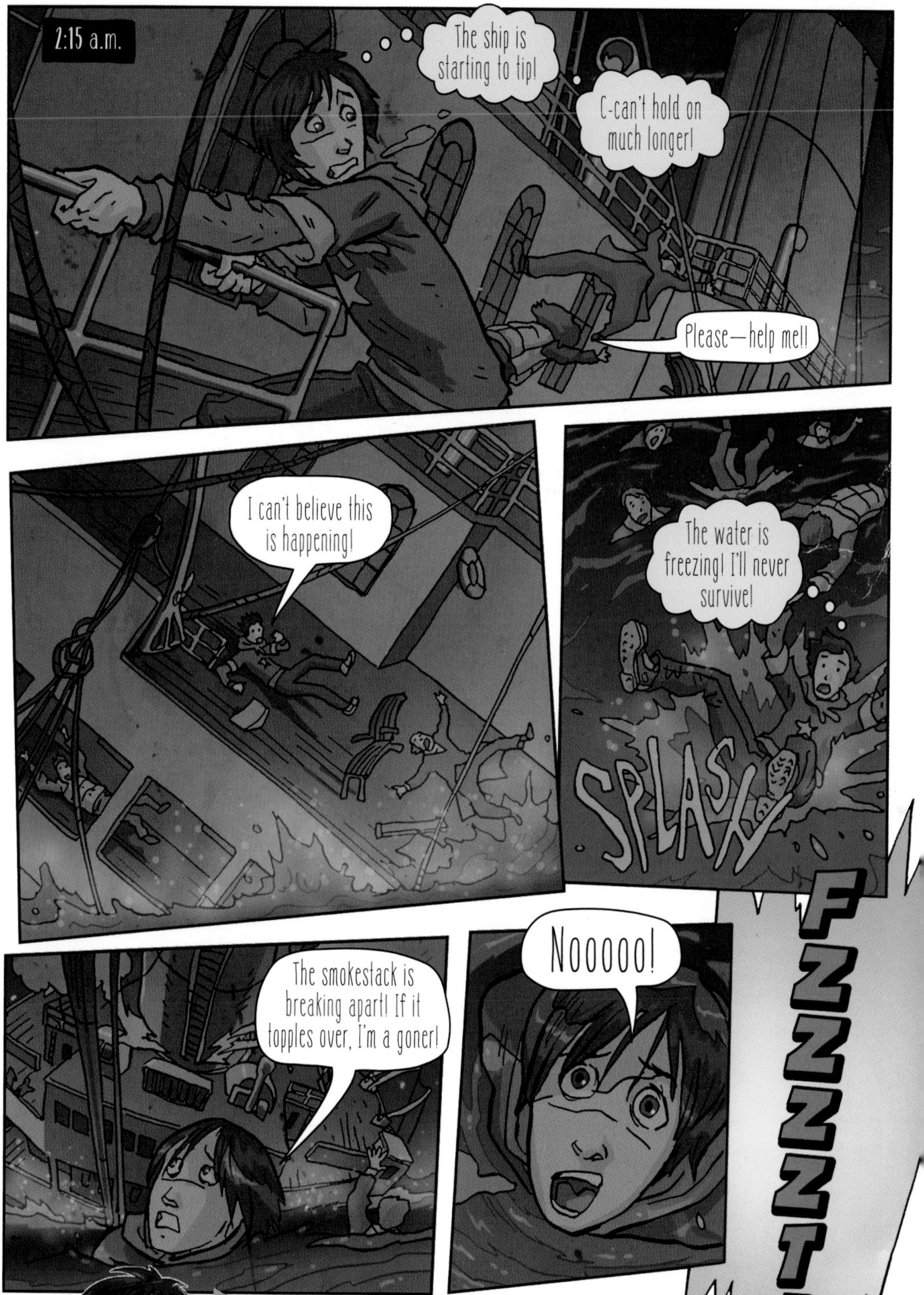
2:15 a.m.
The ship is starting to tip!
C-can't hold on much longer!
Please—help me!!
I can't believe this is happening!
The water is freezing! I'll never survive!
SPLASH
The smokestack is breaking apart! If it topples over, I'm a goner!
Nooooo!
FZZZZZT!

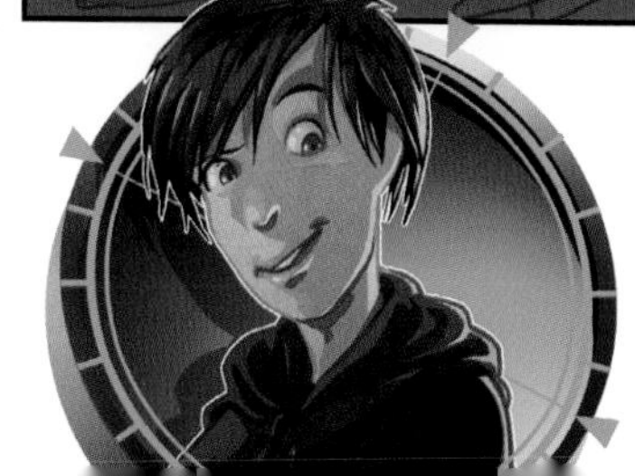

FLUX FACT

The temperature of the water on the night the *Titanic* sank was 32 degrees Fahrenheit (0 degrees Celsius). A water temperature that low can lead to death in as few as 15 minutes.

CHAPTER FIVE

A CHILLING EXPERIENCE

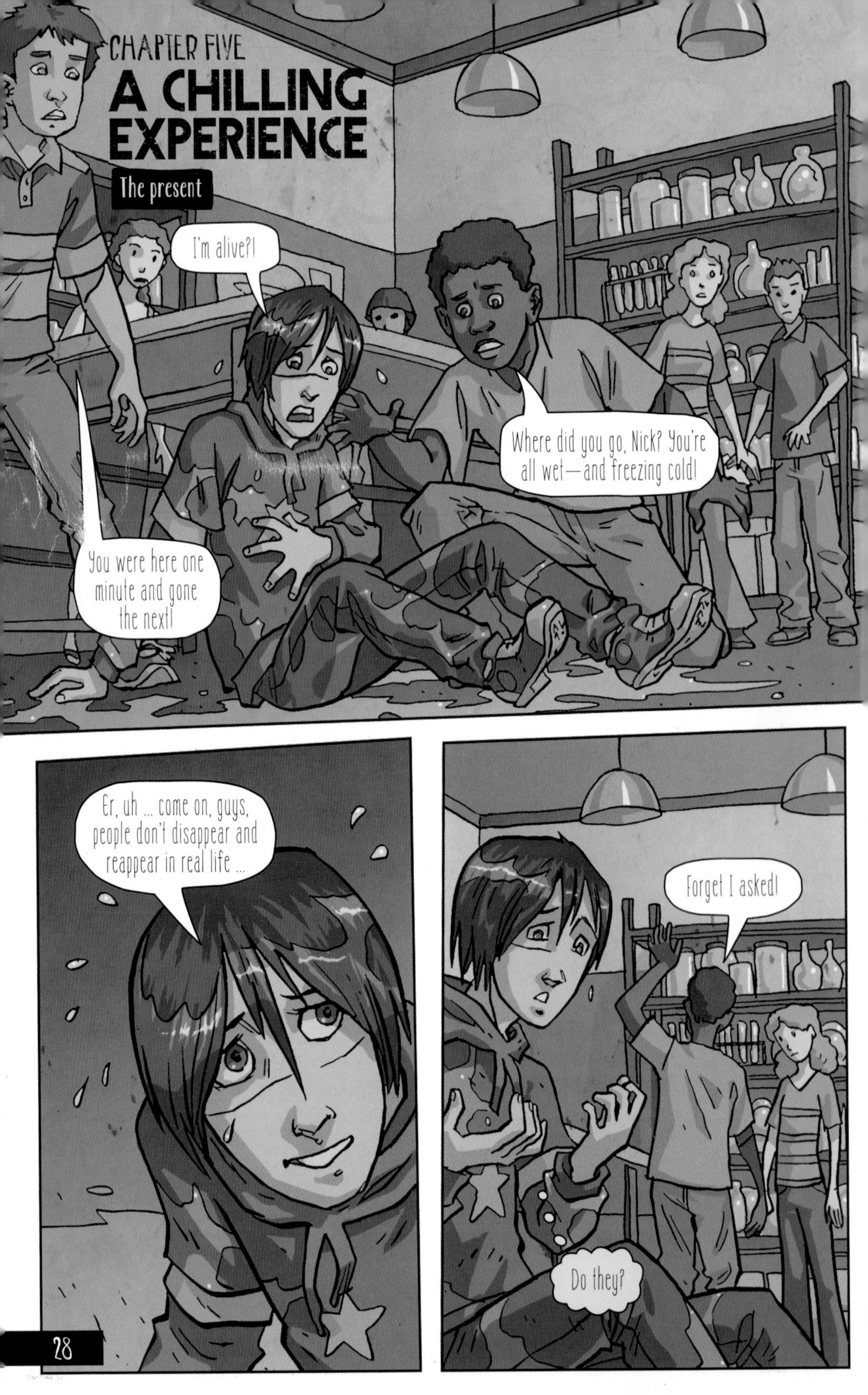
The present
I'm alive?!
Where did you go, Nick? You're all wet—and freezing cold!
You were here one minute and gone the next!
Er, uh ... come on, guys, people don't disappear and reappear in real life ...
Forget I asked!
Do they?

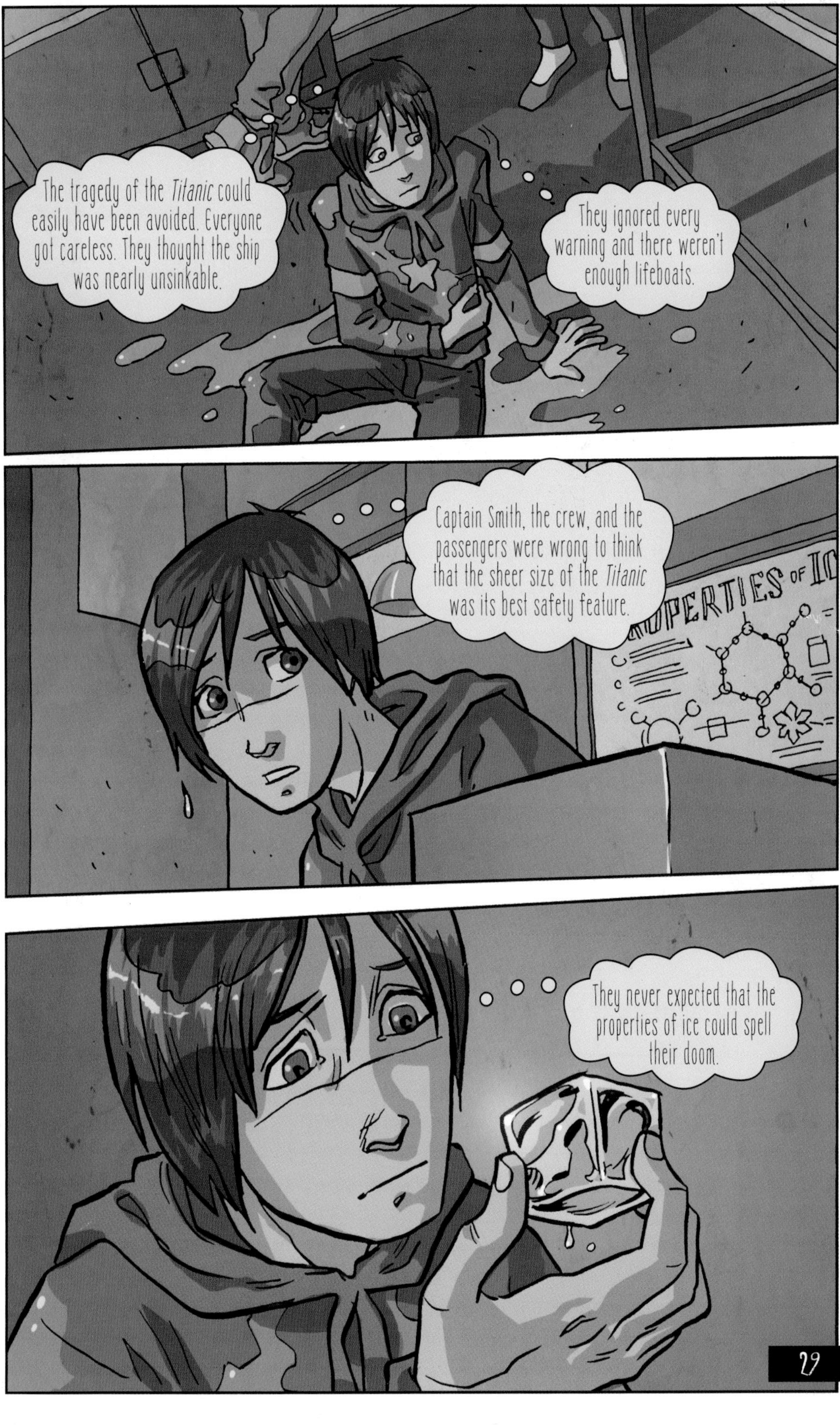
The tragedy of the *Titanic* could easily have been avoided. Everyone got careless. They thought the ship was nearly unsinkable.
They ignored every warning and there weren't enough lifeboats.
Captain Smith, the crew, and the passengers were wrong to think that the sheer size of the *Titanic* was its best safety feature.
They never expected that the properties of ice could spell their doom.

FLUX FILES

BUILDING THE SHIP

The *Titanic* was built by Harland and Wolff Heavy Industries in Belfast, Northern Ireland. Construction began in May 1909 and was completed in the spring of 1911. The ship measured 882 feet (269 m) long by 92 feet (28 m) wide. At the time it was the largest man-made moving object ever built. The White Star Line, a British company, owned the *Titanic*.

PASSENGERS AND CREW

There were 2,223 people, including crew, aboard the *Titanic* on its maiden voyage. More than 1,500 people lost their lives in the disaster. Among the victims were Captain Edward Smith, First Officer William Murdoch, chief engineer Joseph Bell, and the *Titanic*'s designer, Thomas Andrews. Telegraph operator Jack Phillips and lookout Frederick Fleet survived the tragedy.

BELOW DECKS

In the early 1900s U.S. immigration law required ships to restrict the movement of third-class passengers—the lowest class of travelers. One reason for restricting their movement was an attempt to prevent the spread of disease. To follow the law *Titanic* had barriers in place to keep third-class passengers below decks. After the collision no order was given to unlock the barriers. Many barriers remained locked as the ship sank, trapping third-class passengers. Some of these passengers were released by crewmembers acting without orders. Third-class women and children who reached the deck were still placed on lifeboats before men of any class.

WARNING MESSAGE

At 11:00 p.m., *Titanic*'s telegraph operator Jack Phillips received a message from the *Californian*, a nearby ship. The message said that the *Californian* had stopped sailing for the night because of ice in the area. But Phillips was desperate to finish his work on the personal messages of the *Titanic*'s passengers. Phillips ignored the message and did not report it to Captain Smith. He told the *Californian*, "Shut up! I am busy. I am working."

RESCUE EFFORTS

The only ship that could immediately assist the sinking *Titanic* was the *Carpathia*, which was about 58 miles (93 km) away. The *Carpathia* arrived at the disaster scene at 4:00 a.m. For the next four hours, weary crewmen pulled *Titanic* survivors from their lifeboats and rafts and brought them aboard the ship. On April 18, *Carpathia* steamed into New York Harbor with the 705 survivors it had rescued from the frigid North Atlantic waters.

SAFETY IMPROVEMENTS

Governments and shipping companies began making changes to prevent another disaster in the future. All ships were required to carry enough lifeboats for every passenger and crewmember. Communication was also improved. Wireless telegraph setups had to be in operation 24 hours a day. Wireless sets also had to have a backup power source so they wouldn't have to rely only on the ship's engines. The International Ice Patrol was established to track the location and movement of icebergs in the North Atlantic that posed a threat to sea traffic.

GLOSSARY

BRIDGE (BRIJ)—the control center of a ship, located above the main deck

COMPARTMENT (kuhm-PART-muhnt)—a section inside a ship that is divided by watertight walls and doors

CROW'S NEST (KROHZ NEST)—a lookout post located high above a ship

ICEBERG (EYESS-berg)—a huge piece of ice that floats in the ocean; icebergs break off from glaciers and ice sheets.

LOOKOUT (LUK-out)—someone who keeps watch for danger or trouble

WIRELESS TELEGRAPH (WIRE-lis TEL-uh-graf)—a machine that uses electronic signals to send messages over long distances by radio

WATERTIGHT (WAH-tur-tite)—completely sealed so that water cannot enter or leave

READ MORE

ADAMS, SIMON. *Titanic.* DK Eyewitness Books. New York: DK Pub., 2009.

HOPKINSON, DEBORAH. *Titanic: Voices from the Disaster.* New York: Scholastic Press, 2012.

WILKINSON, PHILIP. *Titanic: Disaster at Sea.* Mankato, Minn.: Capstone Press, 2012.

INTERNET SITES

FactHound offers a safe, fun way to find Internet sites related to this book. All sites on FactHound have been researched by our staff.

Here's all you do:

Visit *www.facthound.com*

Type in this code: 9781491420706

Super-cool stuff!

Check out projects, games and lots more at
www.capstonekids.com

ABOUT THE AUTHOR

Nel Yomtov is a writer of children's nonfiction books and graphic novels. He specializes in writing about history, country studies, science, and biography. Nel has written frequently for Capstone, including other Nickolas Flux adventures such as *Peril in Pompeii!: Nickolas Flux and the Eruption of Mount Vesuvius*; *Trapped in Antarctica!: Nickolas Flux and The Shackleton Expedition*; and *Tracking an Assassin!: Nickolas Flux and the Assassination of Abraham Lincoln*. Nel lives in the New York City area.